WIRED
FOR
SURVIVAL

WIRED
FOR
SURVIVAL

The Rational (and Irrational) Choices We Make, from the Gas Pump to Terrorism

MARGARET M. POLSKI

Vice President, Publisher: Tim Moore
Associate Publisher and Director of Marketing: Amy Neidlinger
Acquisitions Editor: Martha Cooley
Editorial Assistant: Heather Luciano
Development Editor: Russ Hall
Digital Marketing Manager: Julie Phifer
Publicity Manager: Laura Czaja
Assistant Marketing Manager: Megan Colvin
Marketing Assistant: Brandon Smith
Cover Designer: Chuti Prasertsith
Operations Manager: Gina Kanouse
Managing Editor: Kristy Hart
Project Editor: Chelsey Marti, Todd Taber
Copy Editor: Water Crest Publishing, Inc.
Proofreader: Kathy Ruiz
Indexer: Erika Millen
Compositor: Jake McFarland
Manufacturing Buyer: Dan Uhrig

FT Press offers excellent discounts on this book when ordered in quantity for bulk purchases
or special sales. For more information, please contact U.S. Corporate and Government Sales,
1-800-382-3419, corpsales@pearsontechgroup.com. For sales outside the U.S., please contact
International Sales at international@pearson.com.

Printed in the United States of America

First Printing August 2008

ISBN-10 0-13-242028-7

ISBN-13 978-0-13-242028-0

Pearson Education LTD.
Pearson Education Australia PTY, Limited.
Pearson Education Singapore, Pte. Ltd.
Pearson Education North Asia, Ltd.
Pearson Education Canada, Ltd.
Pearson Educación de Mexico, S.A. de C.V.
Pearson Education—Japan
Pearson Education Malaysia, Pte. Ltd.

Library of Congress Cataloging-in-Publication Data

Polski, Margaret M.
   Wired for survival : the rational (and irrational) choices we make, from the gas pump to terrorism / Margaret Polski.
       p. cm.
   Includes bibliographical references.
   ISBN 0-13-242028-7 (hbk. : alk. paper) 1. Rational choice theory. 2. Decision making. 3. Social choice. 4. Economics—Psychological aspects. 5. Consumers' preferences. I. Title.
   HB846.8.P656 2009
   330.01'9—dc22

                                                                                    2008023258

For everyone who has the courage to think differently and to make new choices, and for those who are open-minded enough to give us a chance to do so.

Contents

Acknowledgments

No book is written without a lot of help, and this book is no exception. I am deeply grateful to many people living and dead, named and anonymous who have so generously shared their hearts, minds, and experiences with me.

Without Martha Cooley's encouragement and support, this book would not have been conceived or come to fruition. My writing style has been greatly improved by Russ Hall's thoughtful comments. Buck Adams, Pat Donahue, Bob Glauber, Tino Kamarck, Ariel Rubinstein, and Jim Woolsey have been unfailingly generous in providing insight and giving me the benefit of their experience. I am indebted to Glenn Harned and Glenn Lawson at Booz Allen Hamilton for useful discussions on irregular warfare and the artful juxtaposition of quotations that I use to introduce the subject in Chapter 7.

Colleagues at George Mason University and in the International Society for New Institutional Economics (ISNIE) are a wellspring of inspiration and intellectual challenge—in this endeavor, I am particularly grateful to Kevin McCabe, Vernon Smith, Dan Houser, Doug North, Thrainn Eggertsson, and Oliver Williamson. Alexandria and Lee Benham and Claude Menard are consistently and uncommonly generous. Boisterous lunch-time discussions over half-price burritos with Dave Chavanne, Gavin Ekins, Heather Leahy, students, and visitors at the Center for the Study of Neuroeconomics have improved my thinking if not my figure.

New-found colleagues in the Cognitive Neuroscience section at the National Institutes of Health have provided invaluable insights, discussions, and research materials. I am particularly indebted to Jordan Grafman, Aron Barbey, Mike Koenigs, and Frank Kruger.

Alice and Tom Schelling graciously shared a most exquisite lunch and lively conversation in their beautiful home on a torpid summer day. The opportunity to give a colloquium on my work in progress at the Workshop in Political Theory and Policy Analysis at Indiana University in September 2007 sharpened my thinking, while colleagues Jeff Hart, Roy Gardner, Cynthia Rex, Jimmy Walker, and Arly

Williams are a boundless source of sustenance and encouragement. Words will never fully express my gratitude to Lin and Vincent Ostrom, who have literally and figuratively sheltered and nourished me in body and mind since they first adopted me as their graduate student.

Conferences at George Mason University on the Decade of the Mind (May 2007) and New York University on Neuroeconomics (January 2008) provided rich overviews of contemporary research perspectives, useful debate and discussion, and opportunities to meet old and new colleagues. I am especially grateful for wide-ranging discussions with Mohamed El-Hodiri and his family, and his most munificent offer to lend me the use of his camel.

I deeply appreciate thoughtful exchanges with old friends Sharon and Roger Anderson, Mike Fotos, and Claudia Lindsey. Kate Fotos' patience with long scholarly conversations is as admirable as her tenacity defending her hockey team's goal. Last but by no means least, dear friends Rama, Sujai, and rapidly maturing Tara Shivakumar have enthusiastically fed me nearly every Sunday during the past few months as I have pushed out final chapters, providing much needed inspiration, respite, and very sweet amusement.

About the Author

Margaret M. Polski is a political economist with research interests in growth, innovation, regulation, and security. She has more than 25 years' experience developing and implementing transformation initiatives in business, government, and civic affairs. Dr. Polski has a Ph.D. from Indiana University, an M.P.A. from the Kennedy School of Government at Harvard University, and a B.E.S. from the University of Minnesota. She is a Research Affiliate at the Center for the Study of Neuroeconomics at George Mason University and a Research Fellow at the Institute for Development Strategies at the School for Public and Environmental Affairs at Indiana University.

Foreword

When Margaret Polski and I were colleagues in the consulting business I came to regard very highly her extraordinarily informed, creative, and indeed frequently iconoclastic, approach toward understanding how decisions are really made. If you think human beings generally weigh important choices carefully and logically, that we can approximate the key elements of our decisions by using economic models or game theory, that we are basically "dispassionate optimization machines with stable preferences and an objective knowledge base" be prepared for a shock.

Using examples as down-home as deciding whether to help a neighbor by shoveling snow off his sidewalk and as consequential as designing a strategy for counter-insurgency, Polski takes us on a witty and informative trip through the ideas of a number of innovative thinkers about how we make decisions: mind-body interaction, polycentric sensory systems, and strengthening and weakening of synaptic connections. It is quite a ride. My particular favorite (in the context of the author both admiring and critiquing a Monty Python sketch) is her suggestion that neuroscience research is leading us toward a view that our thoughts are "playing around in our brains like jazz musicians in search of a good groove: They may synchronize around a line that is right-on, venture off on some disconnected tangents, or they may just plain get it wrong."

This small book will discomfit more sacred cows and their herdsmen in the field of decision-making than any work written for the general reader in many years.

Brava.

Jim Woolsey
Former Director, Central Intelligence Agency; Venture Partner, Vantage Point, Silicon Valley; Senior Executive Advisor, Booz Allen Hamilton

Introduction

"This is the way the world ends
not with a bang but a whimper."
T.S. Eliot, The Hollow Men *(1925)*

T.S. Eliot was a young American immigrant living in England in the aftermath of World War I when he wrote *The Hollow Men*, a haunting expression of the anxiety and despair that blanketed the inter-war period. Seduced by the sirens' song of global adventurism, the European empires lie strangled by decades of enmity, the near annihilation of a generation of bright young men, economic depression, and the rise of fascism. Across the ocean, the ebulliently prosperous America was too distracted by the roaring twenties to provide solace.

Like many of his generation, Eliot worried that humans would not survive the challenges of modern life. But in this poem, he went even further, contending that in the ways that matter—our ability to think and make good choices—human nature is not fit to survive. We are not only hollow, Eliot bemoans, with "headpieces filled with straw," but senseless. In fact, he concludes, we have already ceased to exist in any way that matters.

Nearly a century later, hurtling into the twenty-first century like some cabbies drive, the sirens sing once more. Shaken by 9/11 and now mired in conflict in the Middle East, insecurity and despair is proliferating faster than weapons of mass destruction. The media and its pundits, old and new, portend demise pointing ominously to signs of global strain: unchecked nuclear proliferation, terrorism, political conflicts, financial volatility, resource pressures, famines, tainted food, and potential pandemics.

Alternately Quixotic or shrewish, citizens are deeply divided. Leaders consistently disappoint. Politicians and business executives spin so fast, they risk vertigo. Analysts and activists dream up vague prescriptions that can't be filled. Policy makers who bother to struggle to negotiate workable compromises find themselves tilting at windmills, dead-locked, or hoisted on their own petards.

Lunching with an artificial intelligence researcher who aims to develop the next generation of security tools, I wondered out loud if we are wired for survival. "It is just a hypothesis—I don't have any evidence," he replied, "but I don't think so." As he sees it, we are hardwired to respond to each other in kind so that if one of us threatens the other, the other sees the threat and ups the ante, leading to increasing escalation and near certain mutual destruction. From his perspective, the world is more likely to end not with a whimper, but a very loud bang.

Thomas Schelling, who shared the 2005 Nobel Prize in economics for his work on conflict and deterrence, sees the problem differently. He wonders at the legacy of our choice to develop and use the atomic bomb in World War II. Without doubting the risks associated with the proliferation of weapons of mass destruction, he observes that we have nevertheless managed to avoid using these weapons in anger for over sixty years. He attributes this result to the emergence of a universal taboo against deployment. But whether self restraint arises from "stunning achievement" or "stunning good fortune," he argues that, "This attitude or convention or tradition that took root and grew over these past five decades is an asset to be treasured," and something we must seek to understand and preserve.[1]

Perhaps we are wired for survival after all. As Schelling reminds us, the story of human civilization so far is a tale of survival. Often harrowing, sometimes ridiculous, occasionally inspiring, and at times, downright incredible, enough of our ancestors have made good enough choices that the human species has adapted. To be sure, our story includes plenty of violence and whimpering, but perhaps our choices and actions need not be as hollow as Eliot feared.

Such Deliberate Disguises

One of my generation's most evocative reflections on survival, choice, and change is the 1972 film, *The Godfather*, which portrays the competitive struggles of two generations of the Corleones, a fictional New York crime family. A classic story of the struggle to reconcile the tension between doing what one wants and doing what one must, the film is part morality tale and part cautionary guide for how to survive intense competition when an old order is crumbling.

The first lesson the younger Corleone generation learns is that survival depends upon picking one's battles and setting priorities. As a grab for control by a rival organization threatens to decapitate the family, their choices sharpen. A trusted executive is charged with eliminating a member of the inner circle who is believed to have betrayed them. Setting off to work, the executive's wife, who knows only that he is driving to the city, reminds him to pick up canollis. Later, after verifying that the hit met its mark, he calmly moves to his next priority, instructing the assassin: "Leave the gun. Take the canollis."

Whether it is with respect to weapons or canollis, intentional choice is what we like to think separates us not only from each other but from the other animals. My cat and I share an instinct for survival. We jump when startled, attend to threats, seek to satisfy our hunger, and respond predictably to cues we have been trained to value. But this is pretty much where the similarities between us end.

Left to her own devices, my cat, who spends most of the day sleeping or watching, rouses herself reflexively in pursuit of prey, the rattling of kitchen equipment, or running water. Although I too have my reflexive moments, I am uniquely able to rouse myself thoughtfully as part of a plan that I imagine will either preserve or improve my current state of affairs.

And unlike my cat, I can, at least theoretically, think about a situation, create alternative courses of action, and put change in motion. When, having abandoned sleep or watchfulness, she runs into the path of an oncoming car and lives to see another day, she does not (as far as we know) wonder at her good fortune, resolve to move to the country, or stop and look both ways before she darts into the road. I, on the other hand, whether in haste, animated conversation, or reverie can (but alas, may not—my companions often remove me from harm's way) reflect on my habits in traffic, seek advice, and make some changes.

Observing my cat and me, you may not conclude that my cat makes bad choices or question her adaptability—she is just being a cat, you may say—whereas you may very well question mine. But should we draw this distinction? After all, despite our differences, my cat and I belong to species that have adapted and survived over a very long time without markedly changing our natures. Devout evolutionists (and hard-boiled economists) argue that competition selects the fittest among us and dispenses with the rest, improving the overall survivability of the species. Like the Corleone's business associates, ill-fitting individuals are sacrificed to sustain the group.

Yet doubt lingers. Those of us who have lived through a few political and economic cycles know the wisdom of the old saw that "it takes all kinds." Someone who is fit in one environment may not be in another. But wait a bit, things change, and this same person may be fit once more. Moreover, the experienced among us know that selection is an imperfect process and mistakes are common. Perhaps you too have railed in disbelief as chance or wrong-headed choices have eliminated someone who is eminently fit.

We have come to understand that diversity is important for survival. But selection reduces diversity, and a prolonged period of bad choices can destroy survivability. Is it possible that we have made such a mess of things that we are reaching the limits of our adaptability, as Eliot despaired and contemporary Cassandras forewarn?

This is where this book comes in. I am a political economist who is interested in developing practical, but sound, approaches to the kinds of choices that global growth is throwing our way—competing in highly competitive global markets; trading energy and the other non-renewable resources that fuel growth; investing in and securing critical trade-related infrastructure such as sea lanes, ports, and airports; addressing the structural impact of global trade; responding to terrorism; or dealing with large-scale natural disasters and health pandemics that can have profound impacts on survivability.

This book is my attempt to come to grips with what we are learning about the brain, choice, and change, and to figure out how we can use this new knowledge to make the kind of choices that will help us survive and prosper in the challenging years ahead. But *nota bene*: These sciences are in their infancy. We are entering a long period of discovery that will yield contradictory results. We must take the evidence with a healthy dose of skepticism while climbing out on a few limbs to experiment. Like any good adventure, this effort will challenge our preconceptions, introduce us to some fascinating characters, and encourage us to learn more.

Here is a preview of the rest of the book. The choices and changes we face today are no less compelling than they were at the dawn of the twentieth century and the differences among us no less severe. Chapter 1, "Under the Twinkle of a Fading Star," describes some of these changes and the challenges they present for how we make choices and govern compared to how we think we ought to. The next three chapters explore how our thinking and choice processes are built and how they function: Although there is still a great deal to be learned, one thing we can say for sure is that we do not think and choose the way we think we do. Remember Monty Python's *Flying Circus*? Well, here is your chance to brush up. Chapter 2, "Bits and Pieces," covers the basic anatomy of thinking and choice. Chapter 3,

"Mind Matter," focuses on the mysteries of conscious and unconscious thinking and choice—and you thought you had something on Pavlov's dog. Chapter 4, "Thinking in the Wild," lays a framework for thinking about thinking and choice that provides an alternative to conventional approaches. Our inventive information handling powers are the subject of Chapter 5, "Feeling Our Way." After reading this chapter, you may never trust your memory or anyone else's ever again, and you may have a different perspective on education policy. Things get even more interesting in Chapter 6, "Mind to Mind," which tackles mind reading—how we understand the intentions of others and the impact of social interaction on thinking and choice. Chapter 7, "Brightening the Twinkle of Our Faded Star," introduces renegade perspectives on security policy that challenge standard approaches, and concludes with some thoughts on how we can use our brains to govern ourselves more effectively in the years ahead.

1

Under the Twinkle of a Fading Star

"There is nothing in the world but change. Our life is only perception."
—*Marchus Aurelius,* Meditations *(170s* AD*)*

It is cliché to observe that we have entered a new period of global growth and change or that we face innumerable threats to our current way of life. The global order we have known for several generations has profoundly changed, and there is no going back: To survive and prosper, we must think differently and make different choices than we have made in the past.

The most telling indication of this change is the trend in global per capita gross domestic product (GDP), which is the value of all goods and services produced in the world, divided by population. Since 2000, global per capita GDP has been rising at the rate of 3.2% per year. At first glance, this may not seem like such a big number. But as economic historian Angus Maddison points out, these changes are remarkable when compared with previous growth spurts.

In the first modern high-growth cycle, which occurred over the period 1870–1913, world per capita GDP grew at an average annual rate of 1.3%.[1] In the next big spurt, which occurred over the period 1950–1973, annual per capita GDP increased 2.9% on average—a jump over the prior period, but still below today's rate of 3.2%. Where nineteenth-century industrialization doubled real per capita GDP in 50 years in the United Kingdom and the United States, China has doubled its real per capita GDP in just nine years.

Current growth trends are particularly interesting because they are the result of changes in the emerging economies, which have been growing at an average annual rate of 5.6% compared to 1.9% for the developed countries.[2] The combined output of these countries, which in recent history have been the least developed and poorest countries in the world, now accounts for more than half of world GDP and nearly half of all world trade. Moreover, together they hold over 70% of global foreign exchange reserves, which is the cash in the global economy cash register.

What does all this mean? History teaches us that rapid, sustained growth and lots of money sloshing around in the global financial system has important implications for resource allocation, geo-politics, and human development. Using Angus Maddison's estimates, until 1820, today's emerging economies dominated the global political economy for 18 centuries, producing 80% of world GDP. But the old world was labor intensive with limited technology or productive investment. Growth was slow and inconsistent, and human development faltered as the vast majority of the world's population struggled just to survive.

Although growth took off with the industrial revolution, the structure of the global economy has been quite skewed. Most of the world's GDP has been produced and consumed by 20% of the world's population, who have resided for the most part in the advanced economies in Western Europe, North America, and East Asia. Life is a persistent struggle to survive for the majority of the world's population, who are ill-educated, often sick, short-lived, and struggling to live on less than $1 per day.

However, old patterns are changing. A leading indicator is the demand for energy resources, particularly oil, which fuels commerce and trade. The emerging economies now consume over half of the world's energy and account for four-fifths of the growth in demand for oil.

Global growth trends raise concerns about the ability to produce adequate energy to meet demand because historically, growth is energy intensive. Maddison estimates that per capita energy use rose eight times from 1820–2001.[3] On the surface, there appears to be little cause for alarm: The geological evidence suggests that world supplies are adequate to manage a transition from non-renewable to renewable fuels. And prices are rising, which theoretically provides both an incentive to invest in production and the means to do so. For most of the two decades prior to 2000, the world price of crude oil hovered around $20 per barrel. Since 2000, prices have steadily but noisily increased to over $100 per barrel.

Yet rising prices have not closed the gap between demand and supply. The International Energy Agency predicts that the world is facing a supply crunch that will push oil and gas prices up to record levels over the next five years. Production is constrained by persistent underinvestment in technology, field maintenance, refining capacity, development of renewable substitutes, regulatory obstacles, geological challenges, and disruptions in supply chains created by shortages in inputs such as equipment and skilled labor, or conflict, piracy, and terrorism.

Although higher prices may be necessary for investing in improving the energy security value chain, they are not sufficient—and they may be a double-edged sword. In the past, high prices have led to rises in inflation and interest rates that have dampened growth. Some estimate that expensive oil may retard growth by 1.5% of GDP. Moreover, prices may not reflect economic fundamentals, in which case they are not a good signal for investment. Energy analysts estimate that as much as a third of the increase in oil prices can be attributed to "political factors."

The "political factors" that affect oil prices create considerable consternation for investors and policy makers. Analysts typically assume that markets form and operate unfettered by government interference. However, the emerging economies and the developed economies are not playing by the same rules.

For starters, few of the countries and firms that control energy production are committed to liberal political and economic ideals. The institutions that are most closely associated with secure participation and property rights, enforceable contracts, and sound financial intermediation reliably function in just three of the top oil-producing countries and in only one of the top net-exporting countries. In the remaining countries, which account for about 77% of world production and about 93% of net exports, exchange is based on personal relations with limited recourse to the rule of law. Moreover, entire regions in the global energy system are wracked by ethnic and political conflict that frequently disrupts investment and trade, and imposes significant costs on transacting.

TABLE 1.1   Top World Oil-Producing Countries in 2006

Country	Production* Thousand Barrels/Day
Saudi Arabia (OPEC)	10,655
Russia	9,677
United States	8,330
Iran (OPEC)	4,148
China	3,845
Mexico	3,707
Canada	3,288
United Arab Emirates (OPEC)	2,945
Venezuela (OPEC)	2,803
Norway	2,786
Kuwait (OPEC)	2,675
Nigeria (OPEC)	2,443
Brazil	2,166
Algeria (OPEC)	2,122
Iraq	2,008

*Production includes crude oil, natural gas liquids, condensate, refinery gain, and other liquids.
Source: Energy Information Administration.

TABLE 1.2   Top World Oil Net Exporters in 2006

Country	Net Exports Thousand Barrels/Day
Saudi Arabia (OPEC)	8,525
Russia	6,816
United Arab Emirates (OPEC)	2,564
Norway	2,551
Iran (OPEC)	2,462
Kuwait (OPEC)	2,342
Venezuela (OPEC)	2,183
Nigeria (OPEC)	2,131
Algeria (OPEC)	1,842
Mexico	1,710
Libya (OPEC)	1,530
Iraq (OPEC)	1,438
Angola	1,379
Kazakhstan	1,145
Qatar (OPEC)	1,032

Source: Energy Information Administration.

At the industry level, over 90% of the world's oil and gas resources are effectively owned or controlled by the governments of producing countries rather than by private sector firms. Only two of the top 15 firms are privately held: Lukoil, a Russian firm, and Exxon Mobil, an American firm. Of these two private firms, only Exxon Mobil, which controls just 3% of global reserves, is located in a country that consistently favors open markets and the rule of law.

TABLE 1.3   The World's Largest Oil and Gas Firms

Firm	Country	Rank	Reserves°
Saudi Aramco	Saudi Arabia	1	300
National Iranian Oil Co.	Iran	2	300
Gazprom	Russia	3	>200
INOC	Iraq	4	>100
Qatar Petroleum	Qatar	5	>100
PDVSA	Venezuela	6	100
Kuwait Petroleum Corp.	Kuwait	7	100
ADNOC	United Arab Emirates	8	>50
Nigerian National Petroleum Co.	Nigeria	9	<50
Sonatrach	Algeria	10	<50
Libya NOC	Libya	11	<50
Rosneft	Russia	12	<50
Petronas	Malaysia	13	<50
Exxon Mobil**	USA	14	<50
Lukoil**	Russia	15	<50

*Proven oil and gas reserves in billion barrels of oil equivalent.
Not state controlled (2). All other firms are state controlled (13).
Source: *The Economist* (2006b).

Every continent and every region of the world has energy deposits. However, primary energy supplies are concentrated in Asia, Europe, the Middle East, and North America (Figure 1.1). Promising new supplies have been located in Africa, central Europe, and North America. However, new supplies include unconventional sources located in deep water or in oil sands, and considerable technical expertise and investment is required to make these sources economically viable. Exxon Mobil reports that over the period 2001–2005, it invested $74 billion on six continents to search for new supplies, build new production facilities, expand refining capacity, and deploy new technologies. They expect to augment these investments at the rate of $20 billion per year over the next decade.

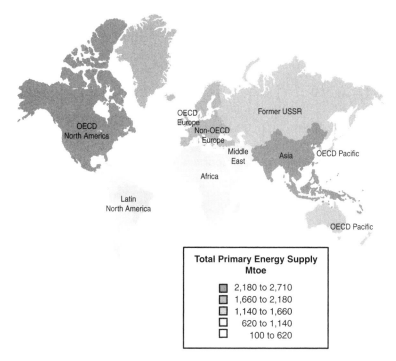

Figure 1.1 World energy resources

Source: Organization for Economic Cooperation and Development/International Energy Administration.

Although most of the world's oil supply is controlled by emerging economies, most of the current demand for energy resources originates in developed countries, which account for 78% of world net oil imports. The technical expertise needed to discover and develop energy resources is also concentrated in developed countries.

There is a mismatch in how exporters and importers think and choose that creates conflict in energy trade relations. Leaders in most of the countries with extensive energy supplies limit who can participate in developing and producing resources, make choices about who will participate based on personal relationships, and are selective—even capricious—about honoring and enforcing contracts with investors and producers. On the other hand, governments in many of the consuming countries require their investors, technical experts, and buyers to promote fair and open competition, make impersonal choices based on merit rather than personal relationships, and consistently honor and enforce contracts. When sellers, technical experts, and buyers have starkly different approaches to the terms of investment and trade, it is the balance of power between the parties that decides how business will be conducted.

TABLE 1.4   Top World Oil Net Importers in 2006

Country	Net Imports Thousand Barrels/Day
United States	12,357
Japan	5,031
China	3,428
Germany	2,514
South Korea	2,156
France	1,890
India	1,733
Italy	1,568
Spain	1,562
Taiwan	940
Netherlands	935
Singapore	825
Turkey	625
Thailand	594
Belgium	583

Source: Energy Information Administration.

Until recently, the balance of power to set the terms of investment and trade has not allowed any of the participants in the energy trading system to strictly dominate the other. Instead, they have been forced to find middle ground. However, as the emerging economies grow and their demand for energy outstrips that of the developed countries, the balance of power favors the emerging economies and their political and economic habits and preferences. This means that resource conflicts among countries with very different political and economic values will emerge, and developed countries will find it increasingly difficult to influence the terms of trade. Because conflict imposes costs on all countries in the global political economy, energy security is a strategic concern for every country, not just those that are dependent upon imports. We can run, but we cannot hide from the effects of changes in the structure of the global political economy.

Harbingers of a shift in the geo-political balance of power are already evident. Leaders in oil-exporting countries have demonstrated that they will use oil supplies to achieve political objectives. Seven of the major oil-producing countries and ten of the top net oil-exporting countries are members of the international producer cartel, the Organization of Petroleum Exporting Countries (OPEC), which was formed to exert supplier power in energy markets. Political leaders in Iran, Russia, and Venezuela have recently nationalized production, reneged on long-term development and production contracts, and strategically interrupted supplies. And China, eager to assure its own access to energy and other strategic commodities, has adopted a "no strings" approach to bilateral engagement that makes it difficult to enforce compliance with multilateral agreements that are designed to open access and level political and economic playing fields.[4]

The recent actions of major oil-producing countries may have a chilling effect on investment in discovering and developing energy resources, which could further constrain supply. This is because discovery and development requires very large upfront investments in the short and medium term. However, returns on investment do not begin to flow until the resource is extracted and delivered to market, which because of the nature of the resource development and production process, occurs over the long-term. If there is a high risk that producing countries will renege on contracts with investors, the costs of discovery and development increase. In the worst case, it becomes too risky for private investors to invest at all (Figure 1.2).

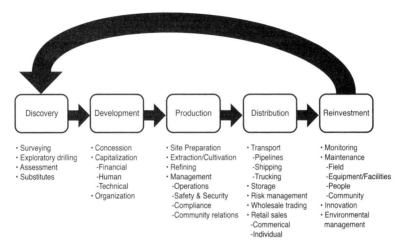

Figure 1.2   Energy security value chain

Disputes over energy are symptomatic of broader differences in the global political economy that are not easily resolved. Just three of the countries in the world are inclined to limit government involvement in economic matters: Australia, the United Kingdom, and the United States. Most countries are either "nanny states," where citizens expect government to play a strong role in the economy, or authoritarian states, which sharply limit political and economic participation rights. Each of these types of states have different approaches to investment and trade relations.

For example, economic decision making in Canada and the Western European social democracies is fairly concentrated, and policy makers take a corporatist approach, which balances government, business, and labor concerns. The Eastern European countries and India have long-standing socialist traditions and are granting participation rights and opening to markets in fits and starts with frequent reversals. There are several devoutly communist countries in the system including China, Cuba, and Vietnam, which aspire to forge a "third way."

But authoritarianism is perhaps the most common tradition in the global political economy, covering the vast majority of the world's population. Some authoritarian countries are ruled by strong individuals, families, or theocracies, while other putatively democratic or socialist countries cycle between military and civilian control. Authoritarian countries tend to maintain relatively closed economies and restrict interaction with other countries.

Different approaches to governing political and economic affairs, uneven patterns of growth, and disparate resources make it difficult to coordinate and cooperate over a host of global security issues that go beyond access to energy. How, for example, can countries with very different values, beliefs, and capabilities address the physical security of territories, critical infrastructure, natural resources, and other common property like the high seas and airspace? How can we protect the personal security of individuals, animal and human health, food supplies, and sanitation, or the security of financial flows and transactions? More generally, as the emerging economies rise, do the developed countries fall, or can we, for the first time in history, find ways to survive and prosper together despite our differences?

Life Is Very Long

Human history is long, spanning more than 10,000 years. However, as the Nobel Prize-winning economic historian Douglass North argues, in all recorded time, only a handful of countries—those we refer to today as the developed countries—have achieved sustained rates of growth and human development. And this accomplishment is very recent, beginning about 300 years ago. Writing with colleagues John Wallis and Barry Weingast, North argues that this experience demonstrates that the key to explaining human development is the transition from a social order that limits access to political and economic participation to one that encourages open access.[5]

Coinciding with the advent of liberalism and modernization, growth has been exceptionally high over the past 300 years. Angus Maddison estimates that world per capital GDP has increased eight times over the past 300 years. This growth has been led by the developed countries, which have slowly opened access to participation in political and economic affairs while coping with any number of changes in the global political economy. Maddison thinks about this progressive opening, or "liberalization," as having two distinct epochs: 1700–1820 and 1820–Present.[6]

Growth in the first epoch, which was dominated by the Dutch, was built on trade and the scientific approach to thinking and choice that emerged from the Renaissance. The nation-state was born. In return for a share of the profits, monarchs granted monopoly rights to private companies. Gains from trade and commerce provided an incentive for elite groups in sovereign territories to improve their terms of trade and the means to develop internal transportation, communication, and navigation. These investments produced some modest technical progress. Political and economic decision making was centralized, hierarchical, and largely authoritarian.

Mercantilism, as this system was called, was nevertheless labor intensive with minimal technology or productive investment, which limited growth and development and created destabilizing social tensions. By Maddison's estimate, average annual growth in per capita GDP in Europe over the period 1700–1820 was just .2%, about the same as the period 1500–1700, which was agrarian rather than trade-oriented. Only a few people could obtain the funds or take the risks required to finance activities that would produce more than a subsistence wage. Wealth accrued to the few at the expense of the many. To participate in the economy, one had to have the right social status, cultivate close personal relationships with rulers, and satisfy their often capricious demands. Even a slight misstep could land a person in dire straights. Labor had very little value and few alternative uses: People could be bought and sold along with the other commodities that filled the holds of merchant ships. Violent political, religious, and social conflicts were common. As best we can tell, life was, in the words of eighteenth century philosopher Thomas Hobbes, "solitary, poor, nasty, brutish, and short" for the vast majority of world population.[7]

Repressive rule and miserable conditions stimulated thinking about political and economic organization.[8] Enlightenment philosophers argued that scientific thinking could be applied to addressing a wide range of human activity to create better societies. They promoted the development of organizations and systems based on reason rather than tradition or superstition. Newton's "natural philosophy," which combined the mathematics of axiomatic proof with physical observation, captured the imagination of intellectuals, producing a new philosophy of science that emphasized skepticism, reason, and the pursuit of new knowledge.

Philosophers and social activists were particularly interested in the nature of government and the limits of state power. The theory of natural right emerged to challenge the traditional theory of divine right. Those who explained social order in terms of divine right believed that monarchs were the representative of God on earth, God granted them the right to rule, and they ruled with divine powers. God was, in effect, an authoritarian social planner who dictated instructions to representatives and maintained order through a centralized hierarchy of command. But those who explained social order in terms of natural right believed that God ruled through natural laws that govern all forms of life. Rulers had the right to rule, subject to these laws. God was, in effect, an inventor who operated through the rule of law, leaving it to divine creations to discover these rules, and to organize and govern themselves.

If one believed in divine right, then human choice should be based on an understanding of God's intentions on earth. Given their special relationship with God, the people who were best positioned to develop and interpret this understanding were monarchs and religious leaders. But if one believed in natural right, then human choice should be based on discovering the natural laws that operate in the universe and using this understanding to develop systems that were compatible with these laws. The pursuit of reason and the development of science and technology were not alternatives to divine inspiration but served and augmented it. Pushing the notion even further, some argued that natural rights included the universal right to participate in thinking about and making choices about social issues. Radical insurgents argued that choices could be made by interested parties reasoning together as equals rather than by authorities: Commoners could challenge the authority of monarchs, and laypeople could challenge the authority of religious leaders.

Challenges to traditional authority, whether in theory or practice, are rarely well-received. The Enlightenment era proved to be no exception. Scientific thinking, the proliferation of Protestant sects, secularism, and the growth of an independently wealthy commercial class posed a distinct threat to the old order, which generated new conflicts and created pressure for new choices.

We Grope Together

The exception to pure authoritarian control through most of the eighteenth century was the English system, which was evolving into a decentralized political economy governed by a marginally representative government. Economic and political matters were governed by a monarchy, a parliament that included representatives of the aristocracy and commoners, law, and a far-flung civil service managed by expatriates and local loyalists. Decision makers increasingly relied on rule by law rather than royal degree.

With England setting the course for the second epoch of liberalization, competition among countries for geo-political dominance fired interest in more extensive change. Public and private discourse thickened with liberal ideas, and laws were passed that created the potential for broader political and economic participation.[9] This opening provided the opportunity to experiment with a historically novel approach to political economy proposed by Adam Smith in 1776. A moralist by training, Smith took exception to mercantilism, arguing that sustained growth would only be achieved if governments allowed individuals the freedom to act in their own best interest.

Resting on a detailed analysis of the vagaries and necessities of human nature, Smith's model of political economy has five features that are the mainstays of liberal political economy: a commitment to reason, private ownership of property and the returns on investment, free and open trade, self-regulation, and limited government that protects private rights, provides goods and services that facilitate trade, and enforces contracts.[10]

Smith's intuition about how his system of political economy would work was simple but powerful. He reasoned that if individuals had the right to pursue their own economic interests through trade and could keep their profits, they would invest in producing things that others want, creating new opportunities for trade. People would specialize in areas of comparative advantage, economies of scale would emerge, and the "invisible hand" of trading activity would guide resources to their most productive use. Increases in productivity would produce growth, which would expand opportunities for individuals, stimulate further innovation, and lead to a virtuous circle of human progress and development.

Taking liberal ideas to heart, the American insurgents constructed an exceptionally daring experiment in economic and political participation. Brashly declaring independence from England in 1776, Americans committed themselves to three ideals: life, liberty, and the pursuit of happiness. They hoped to achieve these ideals by designing rules of the game that protected individual liberty, granted extensive human rights based on natural law, and created many centers of self-governing authority subject to the will of citizens and the rule of law. Central controls were quite limited both by necessity and design, and any attempt to assert authority was deeply suspect. Eschewing colonialism and other forms of imperial prerogative, the newly United States focused on protecting its interests and building mutually agreeable relations abroad, reducing the necessity for trade by meeting more of its needs at home, and improving its competitiveness in trad-able goods and services.

Western countries on the European continent made more modest commitments to liberalism, clinging to hierarchical forms of economic and political organization. Monarchies, social class, paternal authority and other centralized forms of government continued to reign; how-ever, they encouraged policies that favored individual effort, technical progress, and financial and organizational innovations that made it possible to use technology, accumulate physical and human capital, and more efficiently allocate resources. Sources of wealth expanded and diversified—gains from trade and real property were leveraged to create new engines of growth in manufacturing, industry, and related goods and services such as equipment, materials, information, engi-neering and construction, financial services, and transport.

Gradually opening participation in political economies was associ-ated with increased growth. Maddison estimates that per capita GDP increased four times faster in the period 1820–1870 than it did in the entire eighteenth century, increasing average income 15 times.[11] An-nual growth in GDP averaged 1.7% in Europe and 4.2% in the United States, which translated into per capita growth of .9% in Europe and 1.3% in the United States.

But things really began to take off in the late nineteenth century, as accumulated technical progress pushed the western countries ahead of the rest of the world, making them the largest contributors to world GDP. A massive and systematic research and development effort in the United States helped it operate more productively and nearer the technical frontier than other countries. By 1890, the U.S. economy was larger and growing faster than any economy in the world. Over the period 1870–1913, GDP grew at an average annual rate of 2.2% in Europe and 3.9% in the United States, which trans-lated into annual per capita growth of 1.3% and 1.8%, respectively.

However, the course of liberalization was not smooth. The second epoch of change presented a number of challenges. Maddison describes the period extending from 1870–1913 as a stable period of expanding but relatively subdued participation. Suffrage was limited, there were no major international or social conflicts, trade unions and other democratic political activists were weak, labor and capital were flexible, taxes were low, social spending was confined to elementary education and public health, and governments pursued relatively sound fiscal and monetary policies.

Competing for access to resources, investment opportunities, and trade, the European countries expanded internationally by colonizing populations in every region of the world. With lesser means and a deep commitment to the principle of self-determination, the U.S. government adopted a laissez-faire approach to foreign policy, even if some of its citizens did not. Where Europeans expressed their imperial beliefs through statecraft, Americans who held the same beliefs expressed them through privately funded "missions" abroad that were intended to return African slaves to Africa, convert others to particular forms of Christianity, implement religious doctrines such as Restorationism and Zionism, and save or persuade others through health care or education.

But imperial American citizens who ventured abroad were counter-balanced by others who were pragmatic rather than messianic. These Americans believed that they had something to learn from others and hoped that they could benefit from developing mutually beneficial relationships. Internationalists pursued scientific and technical exchanges, joint ventures involving commercial and social entrepreneurship, investment rights, and access to resources, trade prerogatives, jobs, artistic and literary inspiration, and adventure. A timely illustration of how individual Americans' forays abroad influence and often contradict American foreign policy is Michael Oren's fascinating account of the history of American involvement in the Middle East.[12]

But let's get back to our story. Growth and liberalization created structural changes in domestic economies that created numerous dislocations and inequalities. Wealth, incomes, and political decision making were concentrated among those with property and social connections. Participation rights were controlled by small cliques of insiders. For those who were not in the club, poverty was rampant, services were limited, health pandemics were frequent, the environment was squalid, and violence and rude behavior were common. Social safety nets were non-existent so that economic downturns produced ruin from which it was often impossible to recover.

Headpieces Filled with Straw

Hyper-competitiveness, imperialism, and domestic social tensions created immiseration in many countries in the global economy. Global growth slowed over the period 1913–1950, producing average annual growth of 1.8% in Europe and 2.8% in the United States. Growth was dampened by a wide range of poor choices including economic and political conflicts, two "world" wars, economic depressions, protectionism, and other beggar-thy-neighbor policies that emphasized domestic priorities at the expense of common concerns and international order. Ill-considered fiscal and monetary policies and a Cold War with the communist countries contributed to the litany of unfortunate events. Although these developments were very costly for the western countries that were now dominating the global economy, they were even more costly for those countries that had not found a way to consistently grow. These countries, which today are the emerging economies, fell further behind.

The early twentieth century gave rise to increasingly belligerent demands for redistribution and wholesale attacks on liberal political and economic ideas. European and American political economies addressed these tensions quite differently, reflecting the relative differences in their competitive positions in the global economy. Like small ships in a great sea, the European economies were more exposed to changes in the global economy. Following the authoritarian vision of fascism, the socialist ideals articulated by Karl Marx, or the nanny-state prescriptions of John Maynard Keynes, they relied on centralization, government intervention, and social transfers to stabilize their ships of state. The protests of classical liberals like Friedrich Hayek and Michael Polanyi were lost in the howling winds of change.

Protected by a larger and more self-sufficient economy, the goodwill engendered by their hands-off approach to international affairs, and competitive policy-making, Americans took a more laissez-faire approach to social change. Progressive changes in tax, regulatory, and suffrage policies were traded off against preserving private sector control over resource allocation, authorizing few direct social transfers, and creating incentives to encourage the development of local government, philanthropy, and self-help societies. Hayek and Polanyi were well-received, Lord Keynes was rebuffed, and Marxists and socialists were forces to be reckoned with.

Over the period 1950–1973, Maddison estimates that global growth again took off, increasing on average 4.6% per year in Europe, 3.9% in the United States, and 9.2% in Japan, the new member of the developed country club. Chastened by the disasters of the past and heightened demands for independence, the European countries ended colonialism. U.S. partnerships in Europe and Japan stimulated widespread recovery from the devastation of World War II. Extensive multilateral cooperation enlivened liberalism. A host of international institutions and organizations were born to manage crises, international trade, investment flows, and exchange rates. Intensive investments in science, technology, and education stimulated innovation, entrepreneurship, and human development. As productivity soared in Europe and Japan, for the first time since 1890, the dominant position of the United States in the global economy was under challenge.

Growth again slowed over the period 1973–1996. According to Maddison's estimates, average annual GDP increased 2.1% in

Europe, 2.5% in the U.S., and 3.2% in Japan. The period was marked by a breakdown in monetary cooperation and an erosion of many of the factors that helped mitigate price increases in the developed countries. The rise of the Organization of Petroleum Producing Countries (OPEC) forced up energy prices, which contributed to inflation, changes in balances of payment, and structural adjustment. The rise of the East Asian economies in the 1980s contributed to restructuring the world economy and created new impetus for liberal reforms in Europe and the United States.

TABLE 1.5   Average Annual Growth Rates

GDP Growth in Constant Prices
(Average Annual Compound Growth Rates)

Region	1820–1870	1870–1913	1913–1950	1950–1973	1973–1996
Europe	1.7	2.2	1.8	4.6	2.1
USA	4.2	3.9	2.8	3.9	2.5
Japan	0.3	2.3	2.2	9.2	3.2

Per Capita GDP Growth in Constant Prices
(Average Annual Compound Growth Rates)

Region	1820–1870	1870–1913	1913–1950	1950–1973	1973–1996
Europe	0.9	1.3	1.1	4.1	1.7
USA	1.3	1.8	1.6	2.4	1.5
Japan	0.1	1.4	0.9	8.0	2.5

Source: Compiled from Maddison (1997b) Tables 9 and 10.

The breakdown of the former Soviet Union and liberalization in the developed as well as the emerging economies eased many fears about global tensions. However, conflict in the Middle East, the rise of religious fundamentalism, the development of global terrorist networks, resource pressures, and climate change fuel concerns about collective survival. These developments also pose new challenges for how we organize and govern ourselves and our economies. With fewer than 10% of the world's population committed to classical political and economic liberalism, and the emerging economies producing better than 50% of world GDP, one must wonder whether liberalism as we have come to know it will survive.

Writing to persuade his fellow Americans to adopt the U.S. constitution, James Madison argued that "government itself is the greatest of all reflections on human nature."[13] But if government reflects human nature, and we observe different forms of government in the world, why has human nature produced different types of government, and why hasn't there been more convergence as our interaction with each other has increased? What does this suggest about similarities and differences in human nature across the world, how we think and make choices, our ability to understand each other, and our capacity to cooperate for mutual survival?

Here We Go Round the Prickly Pear

Those of us who have been raised and educated in liberal political economies have been trained to believe that it is human nature to make formally rational choices and transact with each other on an impersonal basis in political and financial markets. Price sensitivity rather than adaptation guides our choices, and technical efficiency is our primary goal. The costs of transacting are irrelevant. Providing that governments or bandits do not interfere too much, we believe that if we follow these principles, we will achieve socially beneficial equilibrium in any situation. These beliefs allow us to tell a sensible story about complicated questions—and sensible stories help us make difficult choices. (Some of my colleagues like to refer to this compunction as "faith-based" political economy.) Alas. Although these simplifications may work well in some situations, they are failing to provide reliable predications about global security issues: Energy security is just one example. Instead of making sense, we are making nonsense, weak predictions, and poor policies.

Our understanding of how we make choices and change turns out to be as important as the substance of these choices. Vernon Smith, a

Nobel Prize-winning pioneer in experimental economics, argues that prevailing assumptions and models are grossly misguided. Since the mid-twentieth century, experimental and behavioral economists have been using laboratory experiments to test the predictions of standard models of human behavior. Although their results tend to confirm the predictions of these models in many (but not all) impersonal exchange situations, such as electronic auctions, they are mixed in predicting outcomes in personal exchange. But many of our most important interactions in the global political economy (and elsewhere for that matter) involve personal exchange. These results suggest that we are systematically misunderstanding a great deal of human interaction.

We simply do not behave the way we think we behave. And we most certainly do not behave the way we think we ought to behave. For example, standard models cannot account for the following behaviors that we routinely observe in both the field and in the laboratory:

- Choosing a cooperative solution even if there is a risk that the person on the other side of the bargain may take advantage.
- Cooperating with strangers, and with machines.
- Failing to cooperate or punishing the person on the other side of a bargain when it hurts us to do so.
- Exerting effort or making a contribution without any prospect for monetary reward.
- Achieving worse outcomes when we have complete and common information.
- Forming different expectations and knowledge, even when we have common information and training.

Similarly, standard models—the ones we continue to use and to teach in school, despite their predictive frailties—cannot explain the dilemma Tom Schelling examines, in which intensely competitive and ideologically opposed countries have had weapons of mass destruction for over 60 years but have yet to unleash them. And they cannot explain why some groups are able to protect their natural resources, avert resource conflicts, and avoid the "tragedy of the commons."[14] Nor can they explain why Cuban soldiers protected Chevron's oil operations during the Angolan civil war; why, despite religious convictions to the contrary, some young men and women kill themselves in order to kill others for religious reasons; why on 9/11, an able-bodied man working in one of the twin towers decided to stay with his handicapped co-worker, even though there was no reason to believe that they would survive; or, why many economists—perhaps most—refused to travel after 9/11.

Not only do we not behave the way we think we behave or ought to behave, we apparently do not think the way we think we think. Eliot chides that we are "hollow men ... stuffed men leaning together headpieces filled with straw." But we are far better equipped to understand ourselves and the intentions of others than we were in Eliot's day. Our existing models of human nature, government, and the relationship between them rest on rather thin empirical foundations. This is due in part because until fairly recently, we have had limited tools to investigate human nature. But with advances in the neurosciences and analytical technologies, it may be possible to discover the biological basis of human nature, thinking, and choice.

Wrestling with decades of contradictory research results, it occurred to Vernon Smith and his colleague Kevin McCabe that developments in the neurosciences could be fruitfully applied to developing a better understanding of economic behavior. And so in the late 1990s, with the aid of a creative extension to a research grant from the National Science Foundation, they launched a new program of experimental research that McCabe dubbed "neuroeconomics." Today, this effort has morphed into a challenging interdisciplinary research program that uses experimental and brain-imagining techniques to examine decision making with the aim of building a biological model of economic choice.[15]

As Smith and McCabe were rethinking their approach to investigating behavior, Douglass North was wrestling with a new theoretical approach to understanding growth and change. Steeped in years of research on how people in the western political economies have organized exchange, North concluded that adaptive change requires that our minds evolve.[16] Our ability to form beliefs, develop solutions, and choose among them begins in our minds, which, regardless of how one approaches philosophy of mind, requires at least a nodding acquaintance with the brain. It is human minds working together (or not) that create and enforce the rules that govern exchange, choose among these rules, organize production and exchange, adapt to changing conditions, and suffer or enjoy the consequences.

However, changing our minds and our choices may require changing our brains. Many neuroscientists argue that we cannot change our mental state without changing our brain state. But before we can change our brains, we must first understand them and how they are involved in thinking and choice. Then we must apply this knowledge to developing a better understanding of our own intentions, the intentions of others, and how we govern ourselves and our transactions. Finally, we must translate this knowledge into policy making.

2

Bits and Pieces

"I am in my mind like some people drive."
—*Laurie Anderson, performance at the Walker Art Center sometime in the early 1980s*

No doubt you have had the experience of seeing things in stark contrast to someone right beside you, with whom you thought you shared a common understanding of the world. Sitting together on the beach at the end of the day, one of you sees a beautiful sunset, while the other sees an impending storm. Hearing the distinctive whirr of military helicopters overhead, one of you tenses up, while the other is oblivious. Or walking through a dilapidated neighborhood, one of you senses hopelessness and despair, while the other sees signs of economic development. What explains differences in the way we experience and think about the same thing? And how can we learn to think differently?

Using our minds and thinking about the minds of others is an important part of our experience. We are, particularly in the post 9/11 world, obsessed with "intelligence:" our ability to use information to figure out what is going on, including what others are thinking and planning, as well as what is possible. After all, intelligence is important for survival. Whether we are trying to win or defend "hearts and minds," borders, critical infrastructure, votes, markets, "share of wallet," profits, a contract, a raise, or a little time for ourselves, we are trained to believe that we can somehow change outcomes by changing thoughts and minds.

Although we can probably all agree that understanding thinking and choice is important, achieving this understanding is difficult. Our minds are not only unique, they are quite mysterious and elusive—not only to others but often even to ourselves.

New research in the neurosciences gives us a chance to take a fresh crack at understanding thinking and choice. But to use the findings from these sciences intelligently requires at least a nodding acquaintance with the brain and the nervous system. This chapter describes what we know about our mental apparatus, and how it is organized, functions, and changes over time. Understanding how these systems work biologically is important because one of the ways that we change our world is by changing our brains. Indeed, it may be that we cannot change our world without changing our brains. So, if we want to make change, we must understand our brains. With this in mind, let us take a short journey into the bits and pieces of the mind.

Brains and Russian Dolls

It is difficult to understand the brain and how it functions without understanding the nervous system and the central nervous system, which are the larger systems within which the brain operates and upon which it depends. The relationship among these systems is a little like the ubiquitous Russian doll. The first doll, the largest of the set, is the nervous system. Opening this doll, one finds a similar but smaller doll, which is the central nervous system. Opening the central nervous system, one finds another even smaller doll, which is the brain. Opening the brain, one finds yet another doll, which is the cerebrum. And finally, nested in the cerebrum, is the smallest doll of all, which is the cerebral cortex. Although the pieces in the set are separate, they are not completely independent of each other, for by definition, it is only a Russian doll or a fully functional mental apparatus if there are pieces nested within other pieces (Figure 2.1).

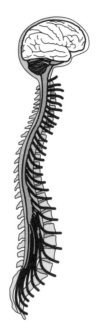

Figure 2.1   The nervous system

The nervous system, and all the systems it contains, is a highly advanced and very complex bio-electro-chemical sensory system that generates mental life, and helps the body and mind work together to warm up, cool down, purposefully act, and keep on keeping on. It does this by linking biological activity at multiple levels and across many different functions.

The major players in the nervous system are called "neurons" and "glial" cells. Conversations among these cells influence the voluntary actions of the muscles of the motor system, which make it possible to hug a friend or thwart an enemy; the involuntary actions of the smooth muscles, heart, and glands, which literally sustain our hearts and minds and keep us in motion; the endocrine system, which keeps the biochemicals flowing that make emotional and mental life interesting; and the immune system, which protects us from disease. In addition to supporting the brain, the nervous system plays a key role in preserving the internal steady state we need to physically adjust to changes in our surroundings and maintain vital functions.

The long and the short of it is that anyone who seriously aims to change their mind or that of another is taking on an enormous and highly individualized biological challenge, which may explain why we have witnessed so many failed reform initiatives. Why? Because to change the way people think and choose, we must ultimately change the nature of the "conversation" among the neurons and glial cells in the nervous systems of the individuals we aim to change—and I mean real biological conversations, not political slogans. As we shall see, this is no mean feat.

No Wonder It's Called a Nervous System...

The nervous system is like a very large and very loud cocktail party, where all the deals in the business of life are made. It is built from and runs on more than 100 billon neurons and perhaps ten times as many glial cells, which are encouraged to communicate by public relations types known as neurotransmitters. Rather dully described by many neuroscientists as signaling and information-processing units, neurons and glial cells pick up information, make a choice about it following some general go/no-go rules, and pass along the information to other neurons and glial cells.

Neurons are the life of the party in the nervous system. The structure of these chatty cells includes a body, dendrites and axons, which extend away from the cell body, and synapses. Dendrites are branch-like structures that transport incoming chat from other neurons. Axons handle outgoing chat. Most neurons talk to each other by signaling through synapses located at the end of both their dendrites and axons. Synapses are a kind of chat room that provides a meeting place for conversation (Figure 2.2).

Neurons come in many shapes and sizes: They may be unipolar (just one axon or one dendrite), bipolar (one axon and one dendrite),

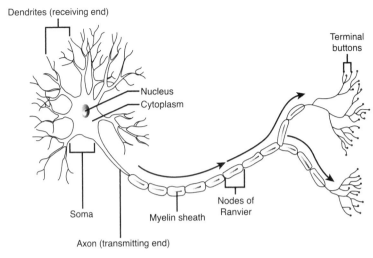

Figure 2.2   Neurons

multipolar (one axon and a number of dendrites), and pseudounipolar (bipolar neurons whose dendrites and axon have fused). Most of the neurons in the brain are multipolar.

The go-to guys who know how to get a party going by exciting or inhibiting neural conversation are the neurotransmitters, which travel in nerve pathways and in the bloodstream. The chemical cocktails they serve up inspire the urge to chat and influence the topic of conversation, which takes the form of electrical and chemical signaling. Although neurons talk out loud to each other electrically, the signal is usually transmitted chemically through the quiet release of neurotransmitters at synapses. Like all good PR types, neurotransmitters know how to keep a low profile.

If you are beginning to get the idea that the nervous system is a pretty wild party, you are right. It is noisy, busy, and very high pressure, providing critical life support 24/7 for as long as we live. When it goes down, we—our bodies and our minds—go down with it. But like all really good parties, what looks like one party at first glance is really made up of a number of smaller parties that are all rocking under the same roof.

Can You Hear Me Now?

Our state of mind—our ability to think and choose—appears to depend on how the neurons in our nervous system are "wired" together in functional networks. Routine exchange among neurons creates regional clusters of networks that grow accustomed to working together to perform specific functions, like specialized circuits in an electrical system, networks in a distributed information-processing system, or individuals, enterprises, civic groups, and governments in a stable political economy.

The neural networks in the nervous system begin to form based on our unique genetic blueprint in the third week of embryonic development. The brain and motor nerves form in the fourth week, and reflexes appear between the eighth and twelfth weeks. The development of intellectual power, which requires massive proliferation and migration of neurons and glial cells, begins during the third through fifth months of development. The formation of routine neural connections begins at the same time and continues well after birth and throughout our life.[1]

But this is not just a nature story—life experience matters just as much as heredity. Neuroscientists hypothesize that while our personal map of neural networks is influenced initially by our genetic code, it expands and become more complex as we develop, respond to internal changes in our bodies, and acquire experience operating in our environment. We become more completely "wired" as we develop, but the wiring changes throughout our lives as we learn, practice our crafts, solve problems, and adapt to change. As we shall see in more detail in later chapters, this means that our minds are quite literally wired by experience, and we cannot expect to think differently if we have no experience doing so.

But let's get back to understanding the biological infrastructure for acquiring the experience that underpins thinking and choice, and open the next two of the five systems that make up our mental apparatus: the central nervous system and the brain.

Mission Control

Many neuroscientists think about thinking and choice as a massively parallel set of neural networking processes that involve many different operating tasks: monitoring the environment to find out what is going on; sensing and perceiving activities and changes in the environment; processing this information and comparing it to memories of our experience; imagining alternative courses of action; choosing a course of action; and acting. These neural networking processes are believed to be integrated in the central nervous system, which is the "headquarters" of our nervous system in the sense that it is a common address for the human enterprise, not in the sense that it is in charge of or directs all thinking, choice, or behavior.

The central nervous system is composed of the brain and the spinal cord (Figure 2.3). The conscious and unconscious actions and output of the component parts of the central nervous system are influenced by sensory or "field" information extracted from other locations both in and outside the body. Field information is conveyed to the central nervous system by the peripheral nervous system, a collection of spinal and cranial nerves. The peripheral system also conveys motor commands from the central nervous system to the muscles.

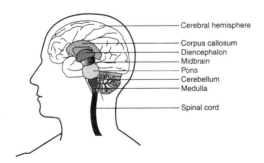

Figure 2.3   The central nervous system

Nested in the central nervous system is our third Russian doll, the brain, which can be thought of as the chief executive officer (CEO) of the nervous system. Like corporate CEOs, the brain gets a lot of attention and often represents the enterprise. However, the real action involved in thinking, choice, and behavior may be distributed throughout the body rather than concentrated in the brain.

The brain itself has three components. Among these three is our fourth Russian doll, the cerebrum, which is believed to be a key player in conscious thinking and choice. It includes the cerebral cortex and the diencephalon, an "in-between brain" located between the hemispheres of the cerebral cortex and the brainstem. The other two components of the brain are less directly associated with conscious thinking and choice. The cerebellum, or "little cerebrum," which is tucked underneath the cerebrum behind the brainstem, maintains interconnectivity within the entire central nervous system. And the brainstem, which is located as its name suggests, facilitates motor and sensory communication.

Relative to body size, humans have larger brains than most animals. Weighing less than one pound at birth, the brain triples in size due to neural chatter about our experience. The brain reaches a maximum average weight of about 3 pounds by age 18, with a range of 2.4–3.75 pounds. It begins to decline in weight after age 50. However, it appears that it is complexity rather than size that matters for cognitive function. As compared to other animals, human brains have more complex neural interconnections, and the area of certain parts of the cerebral cortex that are believed to be involved in higher-order problem solving is larger.

The Real Doll

The fifth, final, and critical component of our mental apparatus for thinking and choice is the cerebral cortex, which is housed in the skull. The cerebral cortex is made up of blood vessels and layers of sheets of neurons and glial cells. There are three conventional ways of thinking about the anatomy of the cerebral cortex: layers; lobes, which are areas of layers; and functions, which are neural networks that traverse layers and lobes.

Form

From top to bottom, the layers of the cerebral cortex include the neocortex (most of the cortex), which has about six layers and many specialized functions; the mesocortex, which are the layers between the neocortex and the allocortex, with about six layers but fewer specialized functions; and the allocortex, which has about four layers and even less complexity. The main functional difference between the layers is the degree of specialization and the complexity of neural layering.

In humans and more evolved mammals, the cortex contains many folds and convolutions, which is nature's way of jamming more cortical matter into the skull and improving connectivity so that we do not have to carry larger heads. Imagine taking sheets of paper, crunching them up in a ball, and fitting them into a rigid form, and you get the idea.

The cerebral cortex has two symmetrical hemispheres, left and right, which are connected by a kind of bridge-like structure called the corpus callosum, and four main lobes or regions. It sits over the top of parts of the limbic system and other sub-cortical structures, which we will explore in due course. Contrary to folk wisdom, there is little evidence that we are by nature right or left "brain" in the sense that we favor or are specialized in one or the other hemisphere: We use both to think and choose, and if one hemisphere is not engaged, we can often shift the action to the other. Although the two hemispheres of the brain are associated with specific functions, they are also able to function independently and duplicate each other's conversations. The extent to which the two hemispheres of the brain are able to function in a disassociated way has been extensively explored by Michael Gazzaniga and his colleagues with very interesting results.[2]

Function

The real action in the brain is in the communication functions that are performed in different lobes in the cerebral cortex. If we think of the brain as a big house party, the lobes are a little like rooms in the house where clusters of neural networks talk together about particular topics. Some members of each network also communicate with members of other networks, like party-goers who drift from room to room, conveying information across networks.

The networks that are involved in planning and executing movement are most closely associated with the frontal lobe. The networks that process sensory information gleaned from other areas of the brain that convey touch, pain, temperature, and limb position are associated with the parietal lobe. Neural conversations about visual matters are associated with the occipital lobe, and auditory matters are handled by networks associated with the temporal lobe.

Other parts of the cerebral cortex appear to synthesize inputs that are believed to be important for higher-level mental conversations, and handle conversations about emotions, learning, and memory. Parts of the neocortex that are involved in higher-order intellectual functions rather than sensory or motor functions are referred to as the association cortex. Emotions, learning, and memory, which are potentially quite important in forming preferences and beliefs, feeling motivated, experiencing satisfaction, and self-regulation are associated with the limbic system.

Areas of the brain that are not considered to be part of the cerebral cortex—sub-cortical areas—also play key roles in thinking and choice. Control of movement, short-term memory, attention, and higher-order mental processes that some researchers refer to as "executive" functions are associated with the basal ganglia. Specialized cells that are interconnected to many other areas of the brain make the diencephalon a key player in mental processes. To establish and maintain attention, researchers think that we have a kind of gateway for sensory conversation and that the thalamus plays this role. Emotional processing and maintaining an internal steady state (homeostasis), both of which are important in thinking and choice, appear to be facilitated by the hypothalamus (Figure 2.4).

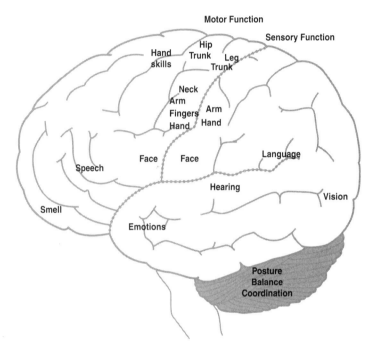

Figure 2.4 Functional anatomy

As we shall see, current findings in neuroscience research suggest that even though the brain is made up of a large number of specialized functions that "talk" to each other, the neural pathways of thinking and choice have not yet been precisely mapped. Although major systems of functions may be broadly associated with specific lobes in the cerebral cortex, lobes have a variety of functions, and many processes and functions appear to involve multiple regions and both cortical and subcortical components. For example, sensory and motor functions are associated with frontal, parietal, occipital, temporal, basal ganglia, and thalamus areas. Social and emotional experience is associated with the limbic system, hippocampus, and the hypothalamus. Learning is most closely associated with the limbic system, but attention and memory are associated with the limbic system, the basal ganglia, and the hippocampus.

Now that we have a grip on some of the bits and pieces and some terminology, let's see how our mental apparatus works in practice.

TABLE 2.1 Functional Anatomy

Anatomical Division of the Brain	Function
Frontal lobe	Planning and executing movements.
Parietal lobe	Somatosensory processing: touch, pain, temperature sense, and limb position.
Occipital lobe	Visual activity.
Temporal lobe	Auditory activity.
Association cortex	Volume of neocortex that is not specifically sensory or motor. These regions receive inputs from one or more areas.
Limbic system, including the amygdale	Emotions, learning, and memory.
Basal ganglia	Controlling movement, short-term memory, and executive functions.
Hippocampus	Emotions and memory.
Thalamus	Relaying primary sensory and attentional activities.
Hypothalamus	Autonomic, endocrine, homeostasis, and emotional activities.

The Brain and Survival

Being able to monitor our environment, accurately recognize a threat, and cope with it effectively is a key survival skill on par with reproductive skill: Without this ability, we could not take the action required to protect ourselves or our offspring. But surviving a traumatic event is a double-edged sword: Although we physically survive and carry on, the experience rewires our brains and the way that we perceive our surroundings, which can affect how we operate and interact with others.

Life in New York City in the weeks and months following 9/11 is one example of how we are rewired by trauma. Less than a month after the attacks on the World Trade Center, I was standing in a desultory morning crowd across the street from the New York Public Library. True to stereotype, we all stood rather grimly defending our small space of sidewalk as we impatiently juggled briefcases, cell phones, and coffee cups, waiting like Olympic sprinters for a too-slow light to change. As we intently monitored the light, a U.S. Army truck pulled up in front of the library. Rapidly shifting our focus to the truck and each other, we unwittingly and uncharacteristically drew closer together, nervously exchanging rueful impressions suspended in a taut human frieze. The air crackled with tension as soldiers began rapidly leaping into the street. The light changed, but no one moved until, to our great relief and utter bemusement, the soldiers began to unload musical instruments. It was an Army band—a threat of an entirely different order than the one we had imagined, but one that caused us to part with the uncharacteristic warmth of shared experience and an elegiac sense of narrow but hardly inevitable escape.

This reaction to the Army band is a very mild example of the type of brain change associated with surviving traumatic experience, which in the more acute form suffered by many New Yorkers following 9/11 is diagnosed as post-traumatic stress disorder (PTSD). These changes and the behaviors that accompany them lead sufferers to misconstrue situations, make inappropriate choices, and otherwise malfunction. People who experience extreme trauma may develop moderate, or severe and chronic, changes in the way that they mentally function. When a significant share of a population suffers from PTSD at the same time, it is reasonable to expect that productivity, growth, development, and the ability to resolve conflict and maintain social order will suffer as well.

Post-Traumatic Stress Disorder

PTSD is a specific kind of anxiety order that can last many years in which traumatic memories or flashbacks trigger the type of stress response that we experience when we encounter a real life-threatening event. Flashbacks are phantom experiences, but they are emotionally intense, disabling, and very difficult to extinguish. A troubling memory arises that triggers exaggerated activity in an area of the brain called the amygdale, which is associated with fear responses. The brain has difficulty suppressing the thoughts that arise with a flashback because areas in the prefrontal cortex and the hippocampus that are associated with attention, intellectual functioning, learning, and memory are "swamped" by the experience of threat and are not functioning properly. As a result, concentration is impaired, and the ability to plan, organize, solve problems, and use calculative strategies is reduced.

Although those of us who experience multiple life-threatening events are more likely to develop PTSD, even among this group, some are more vulnerable than others, and the range of experience varies. Moreover, flashbacks and impaired thinking and choice are not the only effects of traumatic experience. PTSD has a wide and troubling range of symptoms that affect health and productivity, including upsetting dreams and nightmares, insomnia, depression, difficulty concentrating, irritability, hyper-vigilance, being jumpy or easily startled, avoidance, amnesia, detachment and estrangement, a sense of a shortened future, social and occupational dysfunction, higher rates of smoking, and drug and alcohol abuse.

In the worst case, PTSD produces abnormal levels of stress hormones that have the potential to change intellectual ability by altering brain structures such as the hippocampus, or important communications among otherwise undamaged neural networks in the central nervous system. Damage to the hippocampus may lower intelligence, reduce brain substance, or interfere with semantic memory, which diminishes intellectual capacity. High levels of stress hormones may alter neural signaling, distorting feedback to the central nervous system, and affecting perception, sleep, and mood in ways that diminish certain intellectual or social skills. Young people who are still developing physically may be particularly vulnerable to permanent impairment.[3]

Although PTSD is prevalent among those who are involved in combat and other extreme acts of violence, like terrorism, torture, or living in the midst of conflict, it is also common among those who have suffered motor vehicle accidents, crime, abuse, and other types of losses that threaten personal security involving finances, employment, or important relationships. One review of studies on the prevalence of PTSD in the United States estimates that 61% of men and 51% of women experience at least one potentially mind-altering trauma in a lifetime, with a majority experiencing more than one.[4]

Recognizing a threat is an essential survival skill but overreacting to a threat interferes with our ability to adapt and change. Thoughts and actions based on a false or exaggerated sense of threat are inappropriate and perhaps dangerous, harming both the person who is experiencing the threat and the people who are around this person. For example, a common response to a perceived threat is anger and revenge. This is the "fire in the belly" that combatants depend upon once engaged in battle.

But before we launch a fight to the finish, when we are fully functioning, "cool" intellectual neural systems compete with "hot" emotional neural systems to produce a measured response to threat. Cool systems help us evaluate the degree of threat, think up alternatives, consider consequences, calculate odds, ride out difficulties, roll with the punches, and sometimes avoid the situation altogether. As a very astute attorney I once worked with was frequently moved to observe, in any contest there is a subtle but exceedingly important difference between playing "hardball" and playing "dumb-ball."

However, if cooler intellectual systems are swamped by emotional systems, action is less well measured and often counterproductive. Impulsive or ill-considered aggression diverts attention and resources from constructive activity, imposes unnecessary costs, and increases and prolongs stress. Chronically high levels of stress may permanently alter the sensitivity of the brain and its ability to accurately access opportunities and threats, impairing the ability to identify and solve problems and adapt intelligently to changes in the environment.

For many people, investing in reassessing their experience will reduce PTSD symptoms over time if they are not exposed to additional life-threatening situations that replace or reinstate trauma. Three to five days after 9/11, 44% of Americans reported at least one symptom of PTSD. One to two months after, 4% nationwide showed probable PTSD. Although higher rates of PTSD were reported for those closer to the disaster (14–20%), and for those who were actually in the buildings that were hit or who were injured by events (30%), within two months of the incident, the prevalence of PTSD in the cities attacked was estimated at 8%, and the prevalence of depression at 10%.

From a policy perspective, any action that creates or prolongs trauma on a mass scale potentially cuts a society to the quick—even if most members survive. As President Franklin Delano Roosevelt observed in his first inaugural address to a nation struggling to overcome the insecurities wrought by the great Depression, humankind has no greater impediment than fear itself: "...nameless, unreasoning, unjustified terror which paralyzes needed efforts to convert retreat into advance." Engendering fear, whether through threat or action, is the cruelest, most destructive, and self-defeating weapon of all, perverting the most basic human ability to adapt and change, and consigning its victims to a pervasive state of phantom war and cognitive disrepair.

Beyond Bits and Pieces

Understanding the bits and pieces of the mind—neurons, glial cells, neurotransmitters, and neural networks—is important for understanding how our brains function. But the anatomy of bundles of neural assemblies in our brains cannot explain how we think or why we make the choices that we make. As the anecdotes and research cited in this chapter suggest, these assemblies are responding to changes in our bodies and in our environment. To understand thinking and choice, we need to understand how these far-flung and often independent neurobiological networks work together to make coherent choices that reflect the experience of our bodies and minds in our environments. We turn to this very challenging endeavor in the next chapter.

3

Mind Matter

Man (Shocked and annoyed): "LOOK, I CAME HERE FOR AN ARGUMENT!"

Abuser (Surprised): "OH. Oh, I'm sorry. This is abuse."

Man: "Oh, I see. Well, that explains it."

Abuser: "Ah no, you want room 12A next door."

Man: "Sorry."

Abuser: "Not at all. No, that's alright."

(Under his breath) "Stupid git!"

—Monty Python Ltd., *excerpted from "The Argument" sketch*

Monty Python's "The Argument" sketch is a wonderfully hilarious spoof of the human struggle to make sense of and order our experience in the world. As you may recall, the man in this sketch has come to an unfamiliar and thoroughly nondescript office in search of an opportunity to have a good argument. After considering the options, he purchases a single five-minute argument—wisely, as it turns out, eschewing a discounted course of ten in favor of starting with one and seeing how it goes. He pays and is directed by the receptionist to room 12. He locates the correct office, enters, and is immediately greeted by a colorful stream of *ad hominum* attacks. Summoning all the dignity he can muster in the face of this unexpected and seemingly unfair treatment, he demands what he is due, finds he is in the wrong place, and is redirected to the correct office.

However, the man's difficulties do not end with this adjustment. He gamely pursues an argument only to encounter contradiction. As he carries on to another office in an attempt to complain about the quality of the argument he has experienced, the sketch unwinds in an increasingly surreal series of experiences, including being-hit-on-the-head lessons and a complaint office where the attending occupant complains rather than hears complaints. It is then interrupted by various attempts to instill order. The first attempt is made by an officer from Scotland Yard, who charges the players under the Strange Sketch Act of perpetrating "grievous mental confusion on the great British public"; the second attempt is made by an officer from the program-planning police unit, who accuses them of, among other things, ending the sketch badly. With no resolution in sight, it culminates abruptly with the arrival of yet another officer from yet another unit of Scotland Yard.

In the best absurdist tradition, this classic *Python* sketch gives us a window into our confusions and frustrations as we struggle to achieve our goals, comprehend and sort out our experience, and arrive at a sensible conclusion. Although the sketch encourages us to find humor in existential struggle, it offers little hope of achieving resolution. Private enterprise, government, and the rule of law all fail to deliver satisfactory order. Is our experience hopelessly disordered, or can we develop a better understanding of it and perhaps manage it a bit better than the *Python* Players?

As we saw in Chapter 2, "Bits and Pieces," our brains are wired to sense and transmit information needed to function and survive. The way our brains do this is, literally and figuratively, mind-bogglingly complex: All manner of inputs are transmitted at different levels of biological order, across regions and systems, and between our bodies, our brains, and our environments. How do we sense, process, and integrate information about the world we experience, and translate this into action? And how do the disparate neurobiological networks in our bodies and brains work together to think and make coherent choices?

This chapter explores thinking and the science of consciousness or what David Premack has called "theory of mind."[1] Modeling the mind and how it works is an important first step in explaining our ability to think and choose and to think about thinking and choosing. The challenge is to identify the important biological activities involved in the process of sorting out and integrating disparate inputs, identify what can influence these biological activities, and to do all this in a way that helps us understand our experience and make not just better informed but also more adaptive choices.

Thinking About Thinking and Choosing

Thinking about thinking involves studying the nature of the human mind and how it is related to the body. The relationship of the immaterial mind to the material body and the significance of this relationship for defining self and existence—the "mind-body problem"—is an age-old and central issue in philosophy. As you may recall, Descartes memorably framed the problem with his hypothesis: "*Cogito ergo sum*" or "I think therefore I am." In other words, Descartes argued, we exist because we are able to consciously think about existence. But what does it mean exactly to "think," and what is the relationship between our mind and our body in doing so?

One way to think about thinking is as an intentional computational process using specific routines that involve paying attention to, taking in, and processing new information; "encoding" and storing this information; comparing incoming information with memories of prior knowledge or experience; calculating alternative courses of action; strategizing about what others may do; and finally coming to a decision that is logically related to our values and preferences. This is often what we mean by thinking: attending to and being fully engaged in consciously and dispassionately reflecting on an idea or a problem, head on fist, intensely focused, like the model for Rodin's renowned sculpture, "The Thinker."

Standard theories about economic behavior, policy making, and management all assume that we are not only capable of this form of thinking, but that it is our default operating mode, and our brains are able to do so with mathematical and statistical precision. From this perspective, the brain is a trainable information-processing system, and thinking is a set of logical computations. The brain itself is a kind of digital thinking device, somewhat akin to a modern computer, that encodes sensory information into binary inputs that feed rule-based programs or routines, which are our values and beliefs "software."

Yet we know from experience and experimental research that even when we are trained to consciously reflect and plan, we often make choices before we are consciously aware that we have made them based on "intuition" or "gut reaction." Perhaps you have had the experience of suddenly jumping away from the area in which you were situated and, in doing so, avoided being hit by a falling object. You didn't consciously think about doing this. In fact, you jumped before you were aware that you had done so and were not even aware that you were monitoring your environment in such a way that you would notice a change that could startle you into action.

Many—perhaps most—human choices emerge from this same sort of unconscious, spontaneous activity that is not apparently directed by an overtly logic-driven "thinker" or "decider." Rather than thoughtful outputs of logical computations, our understandings of our choices are *post hoc* stories that we weave about what we think we did and why we think we did it. Returning to our example, once you became consciously aware that you had leapt out of harms way, perhaps you speculated that you made this astute move because you heard an intense rushing sound or saw something in your peripheral vision. Because you were passing a building with a terrace, you anticipated the potential for being struck by a falling object and were ready to act. Thanks to the right genes and a disciplined fitness regimen, you had the agility to move quickly and thus avoided being struck. However, although you can make your action sound very logical and calculating in retrospect, the fact remains that you did not consciously make this choice.

If thinking and choosing are both conscious and unconscious, what exactly does it mean to think about something, and what does it mean to have something "in mind"?

Is It All in Our Heads?

A good indication of the limited nature of the knowledge that we have thus far accumulated about thinking is that the people who think deeply and do research on the mind and on consciousness cannot agree on what the mind is, what it means to be conscious, which brain processes are involved, and how these processes are associated with the rest of the body.

One of my favorite characterizations of thinking processes is the *Monty Python* Player's image of a disembodied head that appeared onscreen in between sketches. All manner of things flew in and out, as some invisible man inside this head assembled and reassembled combinations and permutations, mumbling and muttering throughout. In a more elegant but less obvious fashion, and without the help of an invisible man, our brains help us sense what is going on in and around us, segue between events, consider options, integrate sensory information, emotions, and memories, and convert all this into choices. The way our brains do this and the precise location of the action is at present quite mysterious. In large part, this is because it appears that the brain itself does not have this information, and we do not currently have research tools that are smarter than our brains.

Recall from Chapter 2 that with the assistance of molecules acting as neurotransmitters, neurons in the brain receive incoming signals from other neurons located throughout the nervous system and respond by sending out a stream of their own signals. These signals are either positive or negative: "go" (excite) or "don't go" (inhibit). The signals that neurons send are generally related to their perception of signals in other parts of the nervous system. In this sense, our perception of what is going on in our bodies and the world around us is not just in our heads but arises from neural chatter throughout the nervous system.

Let's push it a bit further. If each neuron fires in response to inputs from other neurons by sending out excitatory or inhibitory information to other neurons in many places, then to understand the signaling that is taking place in our nervous systems, we have to consider the combined signaling of many neurons firing with the assistance of molecules connected to other systems in the body. As Nobel Laureate Francis Crick put it, we are a "pack of interacting nerve cells and their associated molecules," and who we are and what we perceive, think, and do emerges from these largely involuntary and transitory neural interactions that occur in response to our experience in our environment.[2]

If our thoughts and choices emerge from interactions among neurons and molecules, then mind and consciousness may be located not just in our brains and but also in our bodies, and our understanding of experience arises from a unified brain and body talking to itself. To see how this may be so, consider that proteins, which are located throughout the body and can form the basis for very elaborate biochemical devices, are essential for neural activity. Upon perceiving a molecularly enabled signal or confluence of signals from other neurons, a single neuron can "fire" at different rates and in different styles. However, it appears that neurons can only send information about how excited they are, and not where they are located, with which neurons they are communicating, or which molecules are involved in transmission. If we do not know to which signals brain-based neurons are responding, we cannot be sure that all or even key neurobiological signals are occurring in the brain.

If we could somehow observe, record, and analyze all neural and molecular activity as we respond to changes in our body and our

world—without disrupting it—we may be able to explain the physiological process of thinking and choice by tracing the pathways of signaling and mapping connections among neurons and molecules. Then
we could speculate about different ways of affecting this physiological
process and run experiments that provide data that either support or
fail to support our hypotheses. Science is a long way from being able
to do this, however, so the next best thing we can do to better understand human thinking is to make estimates based on associations between an external stimulus and a response—this brings us handily to
how we currently measure consciousness and being.

Being Unlike Pavlov's Dogs...

Maybe you remember learning about the work of the Russian scientist Pavlov, who won the 1904 Nobel Prize in Medicine for his contribution to understanding the physiology of the digestion system.
Important as this contribution was, he is equally well known in the
field of psychology for describing the behavioral phenomenon now
known as *classical conditioning*.

Like many scientists, Pavlov conducted his experiments on dogs.
One day, he happened to notice that the dogs salivated not just in the
presence of the meat powder they were fed, but in the mere presence
of the lab technician who normally fed them. Elaborating on this observation, he demonstrated that he could train the dogs to associate a
completely unrelated stimulus, such as the sound of a bell or a whis-
tle, with meat powder, and that this stimulus alone would cause the
dogs to salivate.

One of the abilities that we like to believe distinguishes us from
Pavlov's dogs, or those in our own households, is being able to intentionally and consciously regulate ourselves in our environment rather
than just dumbly responding to stimuli that we have been conditioned
by experience to associate with particular outcomes. Although we do
not at present know precisely which mechanisms are involved in conscious, self-regulated choice, most scientists believe that consciousness

probably has something to do with the ability to pay attention to and retain sufficient information about an event long enough to generate the biological associations necessary to complete a task.

Consider, for example, disorders of consciousness, which are characterized by the extent to which we are able to attend to and interact intentionally and appropriately in our surroundings. The most severe of these disorders is a comatose state, which is characterized by lack of wakefulness, arousal, or purposeful motor response. Once in a coma, our bodily systems begin to shut down, and without artificial stimulation, we die. In a vegetative state, which is judged to be a slightly less severe disorder than a coma, we display an eyes-open wakeful appearance that alternates in a cycle with an eyes-closed sleep state. However, we show no evidence of being aware of ourselves or our surroundings, and without artificial stimulation, our systems shut down and we die. In a minimally conscious state, we can demonstrate clear, although often fluctuating, awareness of ourselves or our environment and, with a little help from our friends and medical science, we can sustain ourselves. We are said to be in a fully conscious state when we are able to consistently function and communicate in a way that goes beyond conditioned or assisted response.

So, consciousness is associated with the ability to regulate and sustain ourselves, and it is currently thought to involve being awake, aware, paying attention, and using our brain and bodily systems to engage in the world around us. Sometimes we have difficulty regulating our conscious thoughts, such as when we ruminate too long on a matter of slim importance or worry too much about events that may never occur. Some people have more extreme difficulties, as is the case for those who suffer from obsessive compulsive or attention deficit disorders. And some significantly misinterpret experiences, as is the case with post-traumatic stress or psychotic disorders. When we have difficulty consciously regulating our thoughts, who or what is in charge of us? Are we more like Pavlov's dogs than we like to think?

Going to the Dogs...

We have only to think of the last time we experienced jet lag or light jag to become acquainted with our Pavlovian selves. Imagine traveling by air from Minneapolis to London on a night flight in March when the days are still rather short. You manage to sleep on the plane and immediately synch your activities with local time upon arrival, determined to make a seamless adjustment and retire at your usual hour. Yet by late afternoon, as the light begins to dim and you participate in a truly interesting meeting, all you can think of is evading others long enough to curl up in an out-of-the-way place and catch a few winks. No amount of coffee or bright chatter can dampen this deeply felt impulse, even though you have had what should be a sufficient amount of sleep to carry you through the day.

Conversely, imagine traveling by air from Washington, D.C. to Reykjavik in June when the light never ends. You get very little sleep on the plane, and upon arrival, you have no choice but to eat breakfast and work, as your hotel room is not yet available. At last, you grab a shower, a change of clothes, and a quick lunch, and you work and socialize at a reception and over dinner without a break, oblivious to time. Despite inadequate sleep and a rather large amount of food in a relatively short period of time, you don't feel sleepy, and you are surprised to discover that you have dined until 10:30 p.m. Leaving the restaurant in full light, you don your sunglasses and stroll back to your hotel with your companions, where you chat in the bar until 1:00 a.m. Still wide-awake but now concerned about the lateness of the hour and the limited hours available for sleep, you retire to your room, draw thick blackout curtains that suppress even the idea of light, and only then are you able to entertain sleep.

In the case of both jet lag and light jag, our bodies and brains are thinking about and making choices about sleep, wakefulness, body temperature, demand for food and water, hormone production, cell regeneration, and other biological activities involved in maintaining homeostasis. Like Pavlov's dogs, we are responding to cues in our surroundings that our brains and bodies are trained to associate with these circadian rhythms. However, until we retrain these rhythms to synch with the place we are in, we will be out of sorts. And being out of sorts in this fashion for prolonged periods is not good for one's general health. But what needs to be retrained and who is in charge?

It turns out that a circadian clock can function within a single cell, and it appears that we have many "clock cells" located throughout our bodies that work synchronously at an unconscious level.[3] Sensing information about the time of day with our eyes and with light-sensitive protein cells located throughout our bodies, these cells begin to chat: Signals are transmitted to endocrine systems located in the hypothalamus in the brain; neural activity in the hypothalamus signals the release of hormones; receptors for hormonal signals, which are located throughout the body, provide information to peripheral biological clocks such as those in the liver. Signals synchronize by reaching a common estimate of the environment within which cells are located. In this way, those parts of our bodies and brains that regulate circadian rhythms take direction not just from our conscious mind, but also from cues in our environment, retraining our bodies and brains at conscious and unconscious levels to adapt to local conditions.

The Mind-Body Problem Redux

Where are we with respect to understanding mind, body, consciousness, thinking, and choice? Although we may not yet know all the processes involved in thinking and choice, nor are we able to consistently associate them with particular neural assemblies, we have enough evidence to say that our "mind" is both a brain state and a body state, which is fleeting but recordable. It emerges from neurobiological signaling that ultimately synchronizes around a common estimate of excitation or inhibition that the brain recognizes as a focal point. We can call this focal point, which is a biological composite of our current and past experience in the world, a "state of mind."

In the course of a life well-spent, we develop many states of mind. For example, if one has experienced New York City and recorded this experience in memory, one can literally be as singer and songwriter Billy Joel wrote, "in a New York state of mind." But because our neural networks are unique, our experience of the world is unique. This means that there are as many states of mind with respect to places, events, and people as there are experiences of life. For some, a New York state of mind may be the comfortable warmth of teeming sidewalks or the edgy intellectual stimulation of an ever-changing scene, whereas for others it may be the anxiety that comes of unremitting activity or the gnawing emptiness of being alone in a boisterous crowd. The pleasure and, alas, at times the pain of getting to know oneself and others is becoming familiar with those states of mind that are most closely associated with who we are in the world as we have experienced it.

This brings us to another interesting aspect of mind: We do not have a single mind, but many minds—some are transitory, some are stored in memory; some are conscious, but most are unconscious. We can entertain more than one mind at once, although perhaps not too well. Maybe you are sitting in a coffeehouse reading this and mentally drifting between the meaning of the words on the page, the emotional experience of the music playing around you, and your own sense of a New York state of mind.

"Thinking," which we can think of as the signaling process that is involved in producing a state of mind, is unconscious. Yet, like setting a top spinning, we can consciously set this signaling process in motion—priming it even—until that transitory moment when it synchronizes around a focal point that produces a state of mind. You can pause deliberately for a moment to consider the events associated with the last time you were in New York, set a thinking process in motion, attempt to consciously guide your thoughts in a particular direction, order them in some useful fashion, and arrive at a seemingly sensible conclusion. "New York is a place for lovers," you may say, because the last time you were there, you were in love and everything you experienced about the city was part of that romance. Or, something in your environment, such as a sound, a smell, or an image, sets your thinking process in motion quite independently of conscious direction. Without warning, you are hurled headlong into neurobiological signaling, become "lost in thought," and are beset by a state of mind. When someone asks you, "What are you thinking?," and you reply that you don't know, you are probably not being evasive—unless perhaps you are in that New York state of mind associated with a lover. In that case, evasion may indeed be the more sensible course. Barring this possibility, it is more likely that you are simply being honest: He or she has caught you off guard before you have had a chance to construct a plausible story for an unwitting neurobiological adventure.

Moreover, as many of us intuitively understand whenever we are overwhelmed by clamor, events in our environments can "drive" us out of a state of mind, interfere with thinking, and make it quite difficult to achieve a coherent mental or physical state. Jordan Grafman, Chief of the Cognitive Neuroscience section at the National Institutes of Health, whose research focuses on the role of the prefrontal cortex in thinking and choice, argues that one of the greatest threats to our ability to think and choose today is the 24/7 digital onslaught transmitted by computers, LCD displays, televisions, and cell phones.[4] Like children vying for constant attention, he speculates that these devices can either prevent us from fully experiencing a state of mind or can drive us out of our minds and interrupt the faculties needed to think critically, make intelligent choices, and sustain a healthy system balance.

The ease with which one can be distracted varies with the input we get from our environment, the way we are wired, and the actions we take to regulate ourselves and our experience in the world. For some, losing a state of mind or a train of thought is, as my golf-loving father often teased, "not a drive, but a short putt." Similarly, as network outages have demonstrated to those for whom their BlackBerry use has become a "crackberry" habit, we do have the neurobiological ability to take control. Rather than slavishly submitting to attention-seeking distractions, we can and, if Dr. Grafman is right, we should master them.

In sum, it takes a whole body—including the brain—as well as cues in our environment to think and choose. Our brain may be necessary for thought, but it is probably not sufficient. From a policy-making and managerial perspective, and certainly from a security perspective, the mind-body problem may be better characterized as a mind-body-environment problem.

If thinking and choice is indeed a mind-body-environment problem, what exactly does this mean, and how does it work?

4

Thinking in the Wild

"The poem of the mind is the act of finding what will suffice."
—From "Of Modern Poetry" by Wallace Stevens

More often than not, we think and choose intuitively, our bodies and brains responding like weather vanes to sensory and social cues in our environment. Influencing and being influenced by what is going on around us, we address our circumstances as best we can with as little effort as possible, relying for the most part on past experience and familiar associations.

One of the clearest examples of this intuitive interaction between our minds, bodies, and environment occurs when we face a threat to our survival. Consider the situation that security troops confront when they are ordered to establish a base in a community that is located in an area where they are not entirely welcome. The ill will of a community is unpredictable and difficult to measure and can take extreme forms, including sniper attacks and hidden explosive devices. Troops are deployed, knowing that it is unlikely that everyone in their unit will return.

As troops advance into the community, someone notices that some local inhabitants are swiftly leaving, and she reports this to the commanding officer (CO). The CO attempts to collect a wider range of information from other troops and his command center, which is located in a remote location. There is no obvious danger yet; the CO orders the unit to fall back and return to its previous position. Reporting his choice to his command center as the unit is moving out, he says: "Something is going on—I don't know what. It doesn't feel right. People are leaving. We are getting out of here now."

The CO has a mind-body-environment problem, and he is making an intuitive choice. He is responding consciously and unconsciously to cues in his surroundings. These cues are producing changes in neurobiological activity in his body and brain. He may wittingly or unwittingly transmit some of these changes to others in the unit, which in turn may produce further neurobiological feedback. All of this signaling rapidly synchronizes around a set of focal points that creates a familiar mind and body state that drives him toward an intuitive choice. With limited time for consultation or deliberation, it is difficult to critically challenge his choice or generate alternatives. The best anyone can hope for is that his intuition is consistent with his mission and the survival of his unit.

Intuitive thinking and choice is, as Wallace Stevens writes, "... the act of finding what will suffice." We re-experience the past and we repeat what we know based on mental maps fashioned by heredity, our memory of our prior experience, associations with similar experience, and our perception of our current surroundings. Sights, sounds, odors, temperature, and social interaction set neurobiological signaling in motion, trigger memories and associations, and summon internal maps that guide our conscious and unconscious thoughts and choices.

Consider our CO. Perhaps an acrid smell unconsciously reminds him of the explosion that crippled his unit at another time and in a similar circumstance. When strangers avoid his gaze, he consciously wonders what they have to hide. His troops are nervous, which unconsciously makes him feel nervous. His "gut" begins to register like a Geiger-counter. With pulse quickening and heart racing, his emotional system automatically flips into "fight or flight" mode. He sees no one to fight except civilians, which violates his terms of engagement, yet he feels strongly that his troops are in danger. *Reason and sensory* experience coalesce in an intuitive choice to retreat to a safer position, where he can plan appropriate strategic action.

Because neurobiological signaling is unconscious, it is difficult to observe or influence. "Satisficing," as psychologist Herbert Simon called this kind of intuitive decision making, is good enough most of the time. If we are well-attuned to a situation and regulating our reactions, intuitive thinking can be a very sound basis for choice and an efficient short-cut. At other times, and often in crucial moments, life throws us a novel play and we must improvise. Innovative choice requires a deeper knowledge of what is going on around us and what may happen in the future: It requires more extensive processing and more energetic calculations than we are accustomed to employing. In novel or counter-intuitive circumstances, our intuition can lead us astray, and yet, it is our default operating mode.

Perhaps if we develop a better understanding of the intuitive interactions between mind, body, and environment, we will be able to invent better ways to augment our intuition and improve both the quality and efficiency of the way we think and choose. We will not quickly discover all the relevant activities and mechanisms at work when we think and choose or what we can do with certainty to influence these dynamics. But we can rethink choice in the context of mind-body-environment dynamics and lay the groundwork for developing a science of intuitive choice.

An Alternative Framework: Intuitive Choice

Standard models of political and economic decision-making are based on unrealistic assumptions about how we are wired to think and choose. All the interesting aspects of life that we routinely consider—whether we realize it or not—are assumed away: individual differences in experience and capabilities; cues in physical and social surroundings; sensations; emotions; bias; uncertainty; change; conflict; and innovation. When we ignore these influences, we misconstrue our own motivations, the motivations of others, and what survival demands of us. Granted, taking all of these influences into account introduces considerable complexity, which is not easy to manage. However, as the economic historian and Nobel Laureate Douglass North argues, political and economic history gives us every reason to believe that we are not only quite capable of handling this complexity and can safely eschew more elegant but less useful models, but the ability to do so is a particular strength of those who have survived and prospered over time.

To grapple with complexity, we need a simple way to think about how cues in our minds, bodies, and environment affect neurobiological processes, and how these processes affect our thoughts and choices. There are a number of useful frameworks in business, economics, and policy-making for thinking about the nature of different types of choices and the impact of physical circumstances and social influences. However, none of these frameworks include what I'll call homeodynamics, or the interaction among signaling activities in our brains, bodies, and environment. What we need is a kind of hyper framework that can incorporate existing analytical approaches and neurobiological considerations. In short, we need a model of intuitive choice.

Here is what I have in mind. Intuitive thinking and choice emerge from interactions among signaling activities in three states: an external state, which includes activities and events in our physical and social surroundings; an internal state, which refers to neurobiological activities that sustain body and brain functions; and a brain state, which refers to the mental maps created by the convergence of neurobiological activities triggered by cues in the environment and the body (Figure 4.1). The extent to which external, internal, and brain states overlap and influence our thoughts and choices depends on how a decision-making situation is structured.

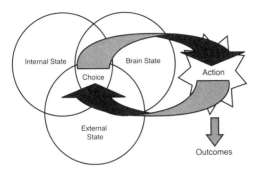

Figure 4.1   Intuitive choice

For example, the three states may be equally important for our hypothetical CO's choice about holding or falling back in hostile territory. His choice to fall back is informed by cues from his unit and immediate surroundings, which are processed and experienced by his body and his brain. But if he were issuing orders from a secure situation room in a remote city, cues in the field—external state activities—would have less influence on his choice than internal and brain state activities. Conversely, if he is ill or incompletely acclimated to his environment, his internal state may have an inordinate influence on how he thinks and chooses. Similarly, if his brain has been rewired by stress and trauma, signaling in his brain may have a stronger influence on his thoughts and choices than either cues in his environment or body.

Let's explore this framework for intuitive choice in more detail, turning first to external states, then to internal states, and finally, to brain states.

Putting Things in Context

Orthodox economists and newly minted MBAs assume that we operate like the hyper-rational Vulcan brainiac Dr. Spock in the science fiction series, *Star Trek*. Spock, as you may recall, was objective to a fault. He sequestered himself among various high-tech logic tools, obsessively gathering vast quantities of data, calculating and recalculating a mind-boggling array of potential actions and outcomes, estimating the costs and probabilities associated with each of the outcomes that could occur, and effectively discounting costs and benefits to present value. Spock's logic tools continually scanned the environment for new information, which they used to update values, assumptions, and other parameters. When he was satisfied that he knew all that he could know and that all his calculations were complete, he recommended actions to Captain Kirk that would deliver the best return to the crew's effort.

Just as Spock was unique among the *Star Trek* crew, there are few Spocks among us when we make important decisions. Curiously, we often distrust the predictions of the logic tools we create to augment our mental capacities. Moreover, thinking in a group does not get us any closer to a Spock-like estimate than going it alone: Behavioral research demonstrates that in threatening situations, crowds are as likely to be infected with what Lord Keynes dubbed "animal spirits" as they are with dispassionate wisdom.

Does a dearth of logical precision mean that we are irrational? Not according to experimental economist Vernon Smith, who earned a Nobel Prize for his research on human behavior. Professor Smith argues that we are "ecologically rational." That is, we make choices intuitively, based on short-hand hypotheses about what we perceive to be happening in the world around us, what other people are doing, and what might happen in the future. As Spock's crewmate Scotty was wont to observe, the problem with the kind of strictly rational analysis employed by mathematically precise statistical and game theoretic models, is that these models often mischaracterize the problem that people are trying to solve, fail to consider important details about opportunities and constraints, have no way to account for change, and misconstrue motivations and incentives.

However, contrary to popular conception, intuitive thinking and choice is fact-based, data driven, and logical. Intuition is informed and structured by a combination of experience and what another Nobel Laureate economist Friedrich Hayek called "local knowledge." Consider our CO and his troops. The more local knowledge and experience they have, the better attuned they will be to their surroundings, and the better informed their judgments and the less likely they are to succumb to what military theorist Carl von Clausewitz called the "fog of war." If they have no prior experience in their surroundings and do not understand what is going on around them, their actions are a pure gamble. They are somewhat better off if they have studied geo-spatial maps of the area, intelligence reports, analyses of the politics, economics, religious life, and other aspects of the community they have entered, sought out first-hand accounts from others who have recently spent time in the area, and engaged in training exercises that simulate real choice conditions. Their chances of being effective improve if they have been engaged in the area in the past, but they are only fully equipped to function effectively if they are acclimated, experienced, fluent in the language and culture, and have a broad range of relationships with people who live in the area.

Because people and choice environments are as unique as snowflakes, sound thinking and judgment requires technical and social due diligence. We are wired to get a better feel for things from what we observe and experience firsthand than from what is written in a handbook or espoused by a group of remote advisors. Think of the last time you had a discussion with someone, and they politely acquiesced while their body language suggested an entirely different point of view, as they ever so slightly lifted an eyebrow, flared their nostrils, or rolled their eyes. We get in trouble when we ignore these kinds of cues in our environment, and conduct due diligence on the cheap or from afar, relying exclusively on technology, regulatory control, or unproven sources. We further err when we imagine that we can overcome adverse local circumstances with a grand plan and strong will.

Foreign security ventures are not the only situations that demand sensitivity to our environment. Taking pains to get a feel for things also applies to more abstract matters such as financial and economic activities. As in war, due diligence in economic and financial matters is more than a paper chase, which can be manipulated rather easily: It too involves looking your counterparty in the eye and getting a good feel for his behavior in the context of his surroundings.

The uncommonness of this commonsense notion about the importance of external cues is illustrated by the failures in due diligence that routinely accompany economic and financial scandals and crises, such as Enron's misstatement of assets and liabilities, or the recent credit debacle. These types of foibles are generally greeted by calls for government intervention and new regulation—as though public officials can stop people from making ill-considered choices. But, as Martin (Tino) Kamarck, an uncommonly sensible executive with long and varied experience in financial services, points out, sound economic and financial choices require extensive knowledge of both the nature of a transaction and the parties involved, which is something that regulation and government officials cannot provide.

Kamarck and a colleague managed to side-step the wild and wooly real estate syndications that preceded the $200 billon Savings and Loan crisis in the 1980s with a thorough technical and "ecological" understanding of their transactions. After an initial technical screening, Kamarck would visit the company that he and his colleague were considering for investment. While pouring through accounting ledgers and financial reports, he would pay close attention to the habits and priorities of company executives and key employees. A taste for luxuries like Rolex watches and private planes, a tendency to favor physical comeliness over competence in hiring administrative staff, and a propensity to emphasize personal convenience over corporate interests—such as relocating the corporate headquarters close to the Chief Executive Officer's home—were red flags that the management team may not have the best interests of investors in mind and an indication that Kamarck and his investors should take a pass on the investment opportunity.

Although our environment provides the cues that help us get a feel for things, we need our bodies to sense and process these cues. So let's move on to a more detailed examination of the importance of internal state variables in intuitive thinking and choice.

Getting a Sense of Things

We are able to experience what is going on around us because we have a very smart, sophisticated, and largely automated internal sensory system that works in tandem with our brains and our other perceptual systems, including sight, hearing, touch, taste, and smell. It is our internal sensory system that makes it possible to literally and figuratively "get a feel" for place, things, people, and situations, and to adjust to changes in our environment.

Think of the last time you unexpectedly found yourself in a situation that didn't "feel" safe. For no apparent reason, you suddenly felt anxious: maybe your stomach churned, your heart seemed to pound, and your jaw tightened. These sensations or feelings are like gauges that tell you that your mind and body have made some changes, which in turn alerts you to use higher-order brain functions to think more deeply about your situation.

What happens when you feel unsafe? Your internal sensing system picks up cues in the environment that your brain interprets as a threat based on past experience with similar cues. Without any awareness on your part, your body automatically initiates changes that rebalance neurobiological signaling in your mind and body so that you are wary and ready to respond to a threat. Your decision to act upon your feelings and sensations depend in part upon the way that you use your brain in this situation.

Like other human systems, the sensory system that monitors and maintains our internal state is made up of millions of sensitive, chatty cells suspended in a kind of biochemical soup that nourishes chemical and electrical signaling. Sensory signaling creates neurobiological maps that provide directions for those members of the nervous system—including the brain—that are involved in serving the chemical cocktails associated with sustaining proper body temperature, blood oxygen concentration, and PH levels, all of which help us think and choose in ecologically rational ways. The importance of our internal state for thought and choice is a bit complicated, so let's unpack it.

Our internal sensory system is made up of several independent systems that pick up and process cues about what may be going on around us and inside us, and help us adjust to change. Sensors in our skin communicate with our fine-touch system, which maps signaling about temperature, form, and texture in our environment. For example, when your skin comes in contact with cold, its sensors send signals that tell your smooth muscles to dilate, which increases blood circulation and preserves the internal temperature you need to function properly. In addition to determining temperature, the fine-touch system allows you to distinguish round objects from square objects, lambs wool from snake skin, or water from oil.

Similarly, as we move through physical space, our musculoskeletal system monitors and transmits signals that help us properly balance and orient ourselves, as well as understand the contours of the physical landscape. It is this system that makes it possible to stand without falling, move around, pirouette, tumble, stand on your head, or traverse a stream by leaping from rock to rock, as well as to reconnoiter our physical location and circumstances.

But what about those attention-getting visceral sensations that overcome us quite unexpectedly: a sense of calm, alarm, "butterflies" in our stomachs, or sexual arousal? Many of these sensations arise from cues in the environment that trigger changes in the chemical profile of our cells and in our smooth muscles. These chemicals and smooth muscles regulate key body functions such as blood circulation, breathing, digestion, bladder activity, and reproduction, which in turn, provide strong sensory signals to think, choose, and act.

In addition to maintaining the internal steady state we need to function properly in our environment, our sensory system plays an important role in how we perceive ourselves and others, our position in

our environment, and how we respond to change. Imagine how difficult it would be to think and choose if you could not "get a feeling" for
a situation or a person by touching, moving through space, or experiencing things viscerally. How much could you know if you lived in a
bubble, and how would this affect your choices? Think of how different it is and how little "road feel" you have if you drive an SUV rather
than a sports car, ski bundled up in multiple layers of clothing rather
than with minimal protection, swim in a wet suit rather than naked, or
meet a stranger by telephone or email rather than in person.

Conventional economic and policy-making approaches assume
that we all have the same body-sensing experiences, that internal
states do not differ in different environments, and that sensory experience does not influence thinking or choice. Yet internal dynamics are
a critical component of thinking and choice, and like so many other
human attributes, there is considerable variation across individuals.
Now let's take a look at the third component of our intuitive capacity:
brain states.

Powering Up

The final, but by no means least important, component of intuitive
thinking and choice is the brain. As Antonio Damasio, Director of the
University of Southern California College Brain and Creativity Institute points out, our brains both preserve and expand our ability to
sense internal and external states and to adapt to changes in these
states.[1] How our brains do this—both consciously and unconsciously—
is one of the most challenging research enterprises in neuroscience.

One aspect of this challenge is to understand what is going on in
the brain in default or "sleep" mode and how this activity changes
when we engage in deliberate, goal-oriented activity, or activity that is
evoked by some kind of internal or external cue. Dr. Marcus Raichle,
Co-Director of the Neuro Imaging Laboratories in the Mallinckrodt
Institute of Radiology at Washington University School of Medicine,
argues that understanding what he calls the "spontaneous intrinsic

functional activity" of the brain is as important as understanding task-related activity. Estimating that task-related neural activity accounts for less than 10% of functional brain activity, whereas spontaneous, intrinsic activity in the brain consumes more than 50% of the brain's energy budget, Dr. Raichle and his colleagues view the brain not as a system simply responding to changing circumstances but as one operating on its own with sensory information modulating the operation of the mind-body system.

When it comes to understanding the role that the brain plays in thinking and choice, the implications of Dr. Raichle's research are subtle but profound. The brain is a real energy hog, consuming over 20% of total body energy. Although many neuroscientists argue that the brain employs a number of energy-efficient circuits and codes—combining analog signals and digital signals in hybrid circuits, splitting signals into parallel channels, eliminating redundancies, using sparse distributed codes to represent information, and so on—the energy required for signaling limits the number of action potentials.

The energy-intensive spontaneous intrinsic activity in the brain that is the subject of Dr. Raichle's research is associated with cycling glutamate. Glutamate sustains the metabolic processes that keep us alive and well. It also functions as a neurotransmitter in the brain; neurotransmiters, which you may recall, are the chemical partners that enable neural signaling. If maintaining system balance expends the greater part of the brain's total available energy, then either our brains primarily operate on the neurobiological equivalent of auto-pilot, or some as-yet-undiscovered mechanism exists that allows us to reallocate brain energy from spontaneous functions to directed functions.[2] In the former case, our environment and our internal sensory systems potentially play a greater role in thinking and choice than we typically imagine; in the latter case, the brain retains its super-power status.

Another research challenge is to understand neural activity in the brain when we are consciously and deliberately engaged in thinking and choice. The goal of this research is to be able to identify which neural networks are involved in particular actions and experiences and describe the signaling pathways that link these networks. This line of research is important because it can help us understand our decision-making processes.

For example, functional magnetic resonance imaging (fMRI) studies, which investigate brain activity when we make conscious goal-directed choices in a very tightly controlled environment, demonstrate that systems in the brain that are associated with social control, emotional regulation, calculative reason, and conflict resolution are all engaged when people interact with each other—even in impersonal financial transactions.[3]

One of the most interesting results from neuroscience studies involving economic decision making is the critical role that emotional regulation plays in making financially rational choices. When we are on the other end of an unfair offer, most of us do what my mother, who it seems was more of an economist than I realized, used to warn against: We "cut off our nose to spite our face" by refusing offers that would make us better off. Studies of people who have damage to the ventromedial prefrontal cortex, an area of the brain that is critical to regulating social and emotional behavior, provide strong evidence that our social and emotional systems can swamp calculative reasoning and conflict resolution systems, leading us to make irrational choices.[4] In short, we do not easily think or choose like Vulcans or economists.

Why might human reason favor social and emotional logic over strictly rational logic? One reason may be that it is more adaptive. True enough, any positive offer, regardless of how small, is an improvement over nothing at all. In the short-term, and from the perspective of a single transaction, it makes sense to accept an unfair offer. However, this may not be a rational choice if we are more concerned with long-term survival than short-term gain.

Consider a world filled with good guys, bad guys, and a-little-of-both guys—a world very much like the one you see around you, observe from news accounts, or have had occasion to experience firsthand. If we want to survive, we need to limit our interactions with bad guys or risk disabling losses. Unfair treatment is a pretty good indication of a bad guy. If we value our own well-being, we learn to avoid people who act badly, and in this way, we improve our chances of survival.

The brain is a necessary partner in thinking and choice. It is active when we think, choose, and act. And when it is damaged, thinking, choice, and behavior are often impaired. When it is severely damaged, life itself is compromised. Although we will not quickly discover precisely how the brain is involved in formulating coherent thoughts, making choices, and initiating action, the search itself promises to be both interesting and rewarding.

Moving On

Measuring and describing conscious and unconscious neurobiological activity is a breathtakingly vast undertaking that many researchers estimate will take more than a generation of research to address. One thing that is clear even at this early stage of scientific discovery is that for the most part, we think and choose intuitively in response to what is going on in and around us. To understand thinking and choice, we will need a science of intuition that can solve the mind-body-environment problem. Our brain, although important, is not the only player and in some cases may not be the dominant player. It is a sub-system in a larger system: We govern ourselves, and we are governed by a convergence of events in external, internal, and brain states. Our brain may be a dominating system in some or all thinking and choice situations—the governor who governs the governors—or it may have considerably less influence than we would like.

The discovery process for developing a science of intuition will involve analyzing the functional requirements and sets of operations that make up the tasks associated with particular choices; identifying changes in neural pathways, systems, neural populations, and cell activities that are involved in performing these operations; isolating the physical and social factors in the environment that influence neurobiological activity; and modeling how all of these activities are organized and governed.

If in fact our behavior is governed by spontaneous neurobiological order, as economist Friedrich Hayek and psychologist Donald Hebb proposed over 50 years ago and contemporary research suggests, where might this order come from? As we saw in Chapter 2, "Bits and Pieces," heredity plays an important role in laying down our neurobiological wiring. However, it is our experience in our environment that creates connectivity among neurons and neural clusters, and generates neurobiological maps or mental scripts that provide directions for thinking and choice. The next chapter explores what we know about how these maps are created and how they function.

5

Feeling Our Way

"...a thread of melody running through the succession of our sensations."
—*Charles Saunders Pierce[1]*

"It was easy compared to the Operational Missions that we flew," claims retired U.S. Air Force Brigadier General Harold (Buck) Adams of his 1974 record-breaking 3 hour and 47 minute flight from London to Los Angeles with Reconnaissance Systems Officer (RSO) William Machorek in a SR-71 "Blackbird." "And," he hastens to add, "We could have really done this in just over three hours—to beat this, someone will have to build a new plane."

The remaining Lockheed SR-71s, renowned as the world's fastest and highest-flying operational manned aircraft, are now retired and on display in a number of museums in the United States. The one flown by General Adams and his ROS is in the Smithsonian's Udvar-Hazy Space Museum in Chantilly, Virginia. An advanced, long-range triple sonic strategic reconnaissance aircraft with tandem seating for a pilot and a systems engineer, the Blackbird was capable of flying at more than 2,000 miles per hour at an altitude of above 80,000 feet: 16 miles above the earth. Developed during the Cold War by Clarence (Kelly) Johnson's Skunk Works to track Russia's development of nuclear weapons, the Blackbird was designed to evade detection and was equipped with cameras that could survey the Earth's surface at the rate of 100,000 miles per hour with enough accuracy to locate a golf ball on a green.

Figure 5.1   The SR-71 "Blackbird"

Source: NASA Dryden Flight Research Center Photo Collection, U.S. Airforce. Photo: Judson Brohmer.

Contrary to General Adams' modest assessment, there was nothing easy about flying supersonic aircraft on reconnaissance missions. Blackbird crews faced extraordinary challenges. First, they were flying the most sensitive aircraft in existence, requiring the utmost precision, hyper-attention, and physical endurance: One false move, and crew and aircraft were finished. Despite constant hydration, crews routinely landed 5–8 pounds lighter than when they took off. Second, they were flying under external cockpit conditions that did not provide enough 100% oxygen to sustain consciousness and with pressure changes that would cause their bodies to explode if their specially designed pressure suits did not function as required. Flying in pressure suits posed additional challenges. Even wearing their suits closely

Figure 5.2   Adams and Machorek disembarking in Los Angeles after their record-breaking flight in the SR-71

Source: U.S. Airforce photo.

fitted, the crew had very little freedom of movement, particularly once they were secured in ejector seats with steel straps that were sufficiently strong to keep them in place should they need to free-fall 70,000 feet through space.

Providing their face masks were clear, they were in the cabin, and they had power, Blackbird crews could see, talk to each other, and hear themselves breathing. Otherwise, they had very limited sensory input: no sense of touch or smell, and aside from instruments, little to see but the curve of the earth and the impenetrable blackness of space. Last, but by no means least, they were spies flying in hostile territory, and there was a good chance that they would be fired upon during their mission.

Flying at Mach 3+ speed leaves no time for thoughtful contemplation. In addition to conditioning themselves for the rigors of supersonic flight, Blackbird crews underwent extensive mental-motor skills training. Using rather primitive flight simulators by today's standards, they practiced procedures under an extensive range of contingencies until their actions and reactions became habit. With limited sensory perception, few environmental cues, and very tight parameters, thinking and choice had to become a conscious, mental rehearsal of learned routines supported by unconscious habits. Crews trained to be cautious, deliberate, and stick to the script: to make continual visual checks or "revisits," and in all actions to follow the mantra: "Do, cross-check; do, cross-check."

It takes a very special person to train for and achieve record-breaking supersonic flight. To qualify for the highly classified program, pilots had to demonstrate that they were superb pilots of exemplary character with "golden hands," and they had to pass the astronaut physical. However, the way that General Adams learned to successfully fly the Blackbird is the same way we all learn to achieve our goals, whether we aspire to break the sound barrier and crack a few windows or skate backward on a frozen pond.

General Adams may have inherited the capacity to learn to fly a Blackbird; however, he could not have done so without training and experience. The wiring we are born with is not sufficient to function effectively in a world in which our brains are embodied in sensitive, finely-tuned, and ever-changing bodies, and our bodies are embedded in complex, unpredictable environments. Once delivered into the world, we must develop, learn, train, accumulate knowledge, and even learn to learn. One of our most interesting properties is that our ability to learn and accumulate knowledge changes with age, training, and experience. Exploring how this happens is our next venture.

Learning Machines

If we were computing machines operating in predictable environments controlled by an omniscient planner, as many of our economic and policy-making theories suppose, we wouldn't need to learn, train, or strive—and experience and age would be irrelevant except with respect to wear and tear. At birth, our planner would program us for a particular set of routines, such as flying supersonic aircraft or playing professional hockey, and launch us into action. If our planner later determined that a change in routine was warranted, it could simply reprogram us. Or, it could rewire us, extending or reducing the range of our routines. With the advance of age, we could be retired, or our planner could continuously renew us with replacement parts and fresh instructions.

Fortunately or unfortunately, these assumptions do not hold in what some of my experimental economist colleagues call "the naturally occurring world." In a world populated by intuitive, adaptive thinkers who roam changing environments with multiple, transient equilibrium, if we are like machines at all, we are more like learning machines than computing machines, and age, training, and experience matter a great deal.

Age matters because our performance capacities are tightly linked to our neurobiological development. From conception until roughly age 22, we are developing, strengthening, and extending our hereditary capacities through training and experience. At age 22 and until about age 55, we are young adults with fully developed capacities, which can be further strengthened and extended by additional training and experience. We are fully adult at age 55, capable of learning, striving, and changing until we draw our last breath; however, our neurobiological capacity to do so slowly diminishes with time.

Training and experience matter because training is how we learn, and experience is what we learn. This means that as our world changes, we need to retrain ourselves and change our experience in order to successfully adapt. From a societal perspective, learning or knowledge production is one of the most important factors in economic growth and social development. Learning produces a social stock of experience that economists call knowledge. Knowledge is associated with the ability to make technical progress. And technical progress—innovation, technological change, and crafting new rules and methods—extends human productive potential, which produces growth and development.

As you may have noticed, rapid change in growth rates in the world economy has put knowledge production on the front burner in public and private life. Debate about reforming educational systems is one indication of our current preoccupation with knowledge production. Other indications can be found in the private sector, where many organizations have appointed Chief Knowledge Officers (CKOs), whose mission has something to do with stimulating and capturing knowledge—or at least marketing an organization's unique ability to do so. CKOs promote "thought leaders," strive to create "learning organizations," and undertake "knowledge management." Academics tell us that it is a very good thing to build "knowledge societies," and many organizations now compete with schools and universities to step-up knowledge production. While accountants are crafting new ways to value the intangible products of knowledge production and attorneys are working overtime to describe and protect this intellectual property, others are seeking to liberate knowledge from proprietary use and create common pools of knowledge—"knowledge commons"—with myriad "open source" tools and approaches.

What exactly does the pursuit of knowledge mean, and what does it entail?

Most discussions of knowledge and learning overlook individual learners and learning processes, focusing instead on proxies for outcomes such as standardized test scores, rates of economic growth, market share, patents, or social progress. Or, the focus is on the *accoutrements* of learning, such as research, prototypes, laboratories, libraries, schools, teachers, and tools, including instruments, books and journals, computers, databases, black-and-white boards, paper and pencils, audio-visual media, and of course, the ubiquitous Internet. However, if we want to improve learning and accumulate knowledge, it may help to take a fresh look at knowledge producers, their products, and their processes.

Knowledge Production

We can probably all agree that learning is a process that produces knowledge. At its most basic level, knowledge production involves a producer, production processes, and products. In nature, humans—individually and collectively—are the chief knowledge producers, and human knowledge production is a set of neurobiological processes that produce memories, which are our stock of knowledge. As very complex adaptive neurobiological systems, we learn intuitively based on elaborate sensory, emotional, associational, and synthetic capabilities that enable us to draw on both our history and cues in our current environment to plan our actions and act out our plans.

From a biological point of view, memories are associations between what we already know and what we are currently experiencing or called upon to re-experience. These associations and the power to associate and synthesize help us survive the present and imagine the future. However, human memories are not physical products like the books, research papers, and databases that we find in libraries and virtual archives. As you have no doubt experienced, memories are fleeting and often elusive; more ephemera than permanent record. For most of us, memories are not so much objective information and facts that we have picked up and archived over time as they are impressions that we are able to recreate from our training and experience in the world.

As in many areas of neuroscience, researchers do not completely understand memory. They don't know exactly what we extract from our experience or how we make or store memories. Like other functions, our memory system comprises multiple systems and structures that handle specialized tasks. The medial temporal lobe assists with forming memories of events and facts, and the prefrontal cortex is implicated in retrieving information. The association sensory cortices are involved in processing sensory and short-term memory activities. Other structures, including skeletal muscle and reflex pathways, are involved in memories associated with acquiring skills and habits. Structures that are involved in perception, attention, and emotion play critical roles. As cognitive neuroscientist Michael Gazzaniga argues, the systems associated with learning and memory are so densely interconnected that it is very difficult to study them in isolation.

The many brain areas that are involved in learning and memory functions are believed to cooperate through interconnected systems of neural networks. In other words, memory—what we learn—is a pattern of connections or associations among neurons that integrates perceptions, emotions, and facts discerned from our training and experience. The basis for this pattern-making process is the phenomenon that "neurons that fire together wire together."[2] That is, physically distant neurons will make synaptic connections if they fire at the same time. As we train and experience events, changes in the strength of the synaptic connections among neurons create what researcher Joe Tsien has called "neural *cliques*."[3] Chatter among cliques forms associations or networks that represent the connections that we form as we function in the world. Learning takes place when neural connectivity is formed or strengthened, and connection patterns or maps are either created or reinforced.

The ability to create, recreate, and synthesize neural chatter allows us to quickly extract information from events, learn from experience, generalize across experience, and innovate in novel situations. However, the patterns of connections or memories that we form are believed to be rather inexact, so that knowing is more like extracting a story from bullet points in a PowerPoint presentation than regurgitating an encyclopedic narrative.

Part recall and part invention, remembering involves getting a bit of neural chatter going across cliques, retrieving a few key points, and then weaving a logical story around them. That said, there is evidence that memory is strengthened by repetition or dramatic effect. General Adams' extensive training to fly a Blackbird is a good example of using repetition to create and strengthen neural connections, forming habits of mind that operate like an auto-pilot at an unconscious level. The persistence of memories associated with particularly vivid or dramatic events, such as the ability of Americans of a certain age to clearly recall today where they were on November 22, 1963, when it was announced that U.S. President John F. Kennedy had been shot, illustrates the role that a vivid context plays in learning and memory.

An important implication of what we know about human knowledge production is that learning processes and products are idiosyncratic, subject to bias, and error-prone. Even though you and I may train for or experience the same event, the way that we lay down these memories of our experience, as well as the memories themselves, will differ, often in significant ways. Think of the last time you and a friend disagreed about a recollection of some aspect of an experience. The reason you have different memories of this experience is that you actually experienced it differently. Each of you came to the experience with different histories, different perceptual abilities, and a different sensitivity to the many things that were going on in the situation. Consequently, you mapped the event somewhat differently by making different neurobiological connections and thus creating different memories of your experience.

It seems clear that we are not really machines of any type—learning or otherwise—but rather we are motivated, emotional, and calculating animals. It is not enough to understand the processes associated with knowledge production. We also need to understand the processes associated with using knowledge to form goals and take action.

Reasoning

Although the ability to reason is innate, the reasoning processes that we use in everyday life are learned—even those that we have no conscious awareness of acquiring. General Adams remembers well how he learned to successfully pilot a Blackbird. Similarly, you may remember how you learned to produce music from a piano, sail a boat, jump out of an airplane, perform decision analysis, or make a perfect *sauce béarnaise*. No doubt both you and General Adams learned to reason your way through these very different activities in much the same way: You were given routines and instructions, and you practiced until it became second nature. But how do we learn to "know" without routines and instructions? How do we know feelings and sounds, such as the feeling of being in danger, the heat of the desert at midday, or the sound of a call to prayer echoing in the hills at dawn? How do we know emotions, like sadness and joy, or the things we imagine? And how do we become impervious to reason, as is the case when we eat or drink more than we should, worry about something that is very unlikely to occur, or ignore facts in favor of fantasy?

Nothing More than Feelings

Antonio Damasio argues that reason, feeling, and emotion are necessarily and inextricably linked.[4] If you think about it from an evolutionary perspective, the economist's ideal of rational choice is not well-suited to adaptive creatures who continually face choice and change—were we to adopt this method, we would get so bogged down in calculations that we could not act when necessary and we would not survive. Moreover, without the capacity to invent, imagine, or reflect on experience, we could not outwit an opponent nor could we evolve or make progress through time.

Instead of emotion being guided by a reasoned assessment of an action's consequences, Damasio argues, reason is guided by an emotional evaluation, which is a learned and remembered association rooted in neurobiological communication. Damasio's assertion that emotion plays a central role in guiding rational choice is not controversial. The controversy arises when researchers theorize about how the reasoning process works.

In Damasio's view, bodily sensations play a critical role, serving as a quick and compelling mechanism for sorting through the many choice options that we confront in any given situation. Bodily sensations are transmitted through the sensory system to the emotional system and the memory system. In this way, sensation and knowledge become imbued with emotional associations, allowing us to literally and figuratively get a feeling for a situation and our options. To get a feel for Damasio's theory, think of a time when an odor or a taste reminded you of a past experience, or how touching something that is soft and wooly makes you feel calm and comfortable. Now think about how experiencing this feeling affects how you are inclined to think and act.

Similarly, Lawrence Barsalou argues that our bodies are extensively involved in knowledge production and reasoning.[5] In his view, knowledge about things we frequently experience is literally "embodied." Training lays down the connections: An event or situation triggers a bodily sensation, neurons fire, and the pattern of firing is captured in an "association area." The next time we encounter something similar, the association neurons fire, which triggers a reenactment of the appropriate neural pattern, and we experience sensation.

A fair amount of evidence can be marshaled in support of embodiment effects.[6] For example, when people imagine actions, such as finger tapping, neurons in the motor cortex, the spinal system, and the peripheral musculature all become active. Similarly, when expert marksmen imagine shooting a gun, their heart rate and breathing fluctuate as if they were actually pulling a trigger. Moreover, when we observe the actions of others, the evidence suggests that an internal neurobiological replica of these actions is automatically generated in our brains through a system of "mirror neurons," as though we were performing the same action.

You can experience Barsalou's theory of reasoning by imagining or mentally reenacting an experience, observing your physical sensations, and assessing the choices you would be inclined to make if you were actually confronted with the same choice. Similarly, think about the last time you cringed when you saw someone enduring a painful experience. On the other hand, if you are a Vulcan or if you have been extensively trained in mathematics, logic, or the scientific method, you may find yourself thinking about the problem in a more abstract way, thereby engaging additional cognitive systems and potentially counterbalancing embodiment and emotional effects.

Something More than Feelings

Nobel Laureate Gerald Edelman also argues that brains are embodied, and that bodies are embedded in particular environments that influence and are influenced by the actions of brains and bodies.[7] However, he takes a somewhat different view of our reasoning process than either Damasio or Barsalou. He argues that biological value systems—the inherited neural systems that release neurotransmitters—play a critical role in creating sensations, emotions, and embodiment effects. Our biological value systems modulate neural firing, which leads to more or less firing, and changes in the connectivity among neurons. These systems function as first-order, internal, neurobiological rules of the game. Examples of biological value system activity include the release of adrenaline in response to being startled, dopamine in connection with the experience of reward and punishment, serotonin with respect to mood, and acetylcholine in connection with waking and sleeping.

In Edelman's view, the brain is not evolved for knowledge production *per se* but for the elaboration of knowledge. He thinks about the brain as an advanced selection system. Noting that distant neurons will make synaptic connections if their firing patterns are temporarily correlated, he argues that training produces signals that either strengthen or weaken synaptic connections and signal pathways, favoring some circuits over others. Continuous, constantly changing signaling within and across brain regions leads to synchronized firing of neurons in particular circuits. In "use it or lose it" fashion, synchronization selects out those firing patterns that are not synchronized, providing a coherent, coordinated pattern of engagement of neural circuits. From this perspective, learning is a process in which the brain is speaking to itself, and memory or knowledge is a synchronized re-categorization of perceptually based neurobiological activity that is critically influenced by biological value systems.

Although there is still much to be learned about our reasoning processes, there are several propositions for which there is consider-able consensus. First, our brains do not operate according to formal rules of logic, although they are capable of learning and employing logical systems. Our primary mode of reasoning is pattern recognition, which gives us substantial latitude to create and to adapt to novel sit-uations. Second, as Edelman puts it, our brains are embodied and our bodies are embedded in particular environments. This means that our thoughts and choices emerge from an intuitive interaction between brain, body, and environmental states. As a consequence, human rea-soning trades off precision for rapid, associative power, which means that it is error-prone and subject to bias.

Flying Circus on Steroids

Thinking about errors and biases in the human reasoning process, I am again reminded of the *Monty Python* Players' image of a disem-bodied head that appeared onscreen in between sketches in the "Fly-ing Circus." Although the *Pythons* imagined thoughts flying in and out of our brains under the direction of an invisible conductor, the neuro-science research suggests that a better image may be one of thoughts playing around inside our brains like jazz musicians in search of a good groove: They may synchronize along a line that is right-on, venture off on some disconnected tangents, or they may just plain get it wrong.

The way most of us think about security is a good example of some of the frailties in our reasoning process. Bruce Schneier points out that often the first mistake we make in dealing with security problems is that we frame security in terms of threats rather than trade-offs.[5] We lose some money on a stock investment, and rather than calculating changes in the value of our entire portfolio of assets over time, we panic and withdraw from the market altogether. We pay more to buy warranty insurance on an electronic device than it is likely to cost to replace it should it fail. Or we drive a car to a remote destination because we are afraid to fly, even though the probability of being injured or killed in a car accident is many times greater than that of an airplane accident.

Pointing to research in behavioral economics and the psychology of risk and decision-making, Schneier argues that we often make seemingly illogical security choices because we fail to reconcile our "feelings" about security with the mathematical "reality" of security, which causes our estimations of risk to run amok. On a fairly systematic basis, we tend to exaggerate spectacular but unlikely risks and downplay common risks. We have trouble estimating risks in unusual situations. Risks that affect us personally appear to us to be greater than risks that affect others. We underestimate risks we willingly take and overestimate risks in situations we can't control. We overestimate risks that are widely and publicly discussed.

Surveying a broad range of research in cognitive neuroscience, John Cacioppo and Gary Berntson identify a number of biases in the way we reason that get in the way of strictly logical decision making.[9] We tend to search for information that confirms what we already believe to be true and block out information that challenges our existing beliefs. We consistently overestimate the probability that a desired event is likely to occur, the importance of our own contribution, and the pervasiveness of our own beliefs, whereas we underestimate the risks associated with our actions. We rationalize more than we reason, and our memories are more likely to be biased reconstructions than accurate recollections of events. Our ability to mentally simulate events can substantially influence our thoughts and choices, lead us to mix fact with fantasy, and fuel our tendency toward self-deception.

Our biases are innate, pervasive, and automatic. They emerge not from disembodied brains but from brain-body-environment interactions and the intuitive way that we reason. Heredity, experience, training, sensations, emotions, brain anatomy, physical circumstances, and the presence of others affect thinking and choice in ways that are not predicted by Bayesian logic. Our past and our biases are sources of friction that tend to lock us into status quo routines, and our tendency to reason based on the gist of things makes it difficult for us to work with detailed information. We are efficient but imperfect interpreters, skimming our biased stock of knowledge to conjure theories about our environment and the courses of action that will lead to instinctively preferred results.

Yet unlike other primates, we can overcome our biases and reduce our susceptibility to unwitting influence. If motivated to do so, we can "tune-out" or discount cues in our environment, delay gratification, augment our innate capabilities using tools and technologies, and consciously direct thinking and choice processes. We can seek contradictory evidence, grapple with differences, think ahead, plan, and choose to act because we wish to accomplish particular goals or satisfy specific interests. Although we can and often do take shortcuts and act based on instinct and habit, we can draw on the same elaborate sensory, memory, reasoning, and emotional capabilities to consciously plan and launch a new venture or try a fresh approach. But to do so requires an understanding of motivation, which brings us handily to Chapter 6, "Mind to Mind."

6

Mind to Mind

"If Sally jumped off a cliff, would you?"
—*My mother, who—thanks to an armed rhetorical
strategy—has little cause to rest in anything other
than peace.*

"Groupthink" and the social conformity it represents are endemic in every sphere of human thinking and choice. Apple Computer's 1984 Super Bowl commercial, "1984," which launched the Macintosh personal computer, is one of the most admired and persistent marketing campaigns in advertising history. Inspired by George Orwell's classic social science fiction novel, *1984*, the commercial portrays the market entry of the Mac as a heroic opportunity to eschew social conformity by rejecting the ascending IBM PC and PC compatibles.

In the commercial, a woman wearing Apple-red running shorts and carrying a sledgehammer is being chased by security guards through a large industrial hall filled with vacuous souls in drab coveralls who are uniformly seated on benches facing an enormous video screen. As she runs toward the screen, a Big Brother-like video image intones:

> "Today, we celebrate the first glorious anniversary of the Information Purification Directives. We have created, for the first time in all history, a garden of pure ideology, where each worker may bloom, secure from the pests purveying contradictory thoughts. Our Unification of Thought is more powerful a weapon than any fleet or army on earth. We are one

people, with one will, one resolve, one cause. Our enemies shall talk themselves to death and we will bury them with their own confusion. We shall prevail!"

In the final moment, the woman hurls the sledgehammer at the screen as though she were throwing a discus, smashing it, and the thought control it represents, to pieces. An announcer proclaims:

"On January 24th, Apple Computer will introduce Macintosh. And you'll see why 1984 won't be like '1984'."

Launching Macintosh Office in 1985, Apple followed up with another infamous Super Bowl commercial, entitled "Lemmings." In this vignette, a seemingly endless line of blindfolded business men in gray flannel suits carrying briefcases and marching to an ominous version of the work song "Heigh-Ho" make their way through a desolate landscape to the edge of a cliff, where one by one they plummet headlong to their doom. A voiceover announces that Macintosh Office will soon come to market, causing the next businessman to reach the brink to pause briefly. The announcer suggests "looking into it," and the businessman cautiously uncovers one eye to survey the scene before him. As a new influx of willing victims approaches, the announcer gamely proclaims: "Or you can go on with business as usual."

Despite this entertaining, provocative, and award-winning promotional assault on the personal computing market, Apple failed to stem the ascent of the PC, which steadily captured market share, reaching about 97% by the 1990s. Although Apple has established and maintained a small maverick niche, to grow it has had to invent new products to secure its own first mover stranglehold on consumer hearts and minds. Celebrating the twentieth anniversary of the Macintosh at the 2004 MacWorld Expo, Steve Jobs played an updated version of the "1984" commercial in which the heroine is equipped with an iPod and white earbuds.

Social conformity is a perplexing phenomenon not just for business people who are trying to win market share, but also for policy makers who struggle to understand the motivations of others and how to influence these motivations for the common good. In this chapter, we explore the nature of motivation and the role of social interaction in thinking and choice.

Reflecting on what we have learned about the way that we think and choose, perhaps you can see why groupthink is so pervasive. First, we don't have much spare mental energy: With just 20–40% of brain energy available at any given time to work on challenges other than maintaining system balance, in the short run it is efficient to adopt mental shortcuts and "follow the crowd." Aching under the weight of the six-pound PC laptop slung over your shoulder and with visions of rotator cuff surgery dancing in your head, you may long to replace it with the new ultra-thin Mac, but to do so requires a significant investment in learning to navigate a new operating system and alternative software. Even calculating the potential return on investing your time to make this transition is costly, and so, as the song says, "heigh-ho, heigh-ho, it's off to work we go"—nothing new ventured, and nothing new gained.

Second, social conformity can be an evolutionarily rational strategy. We depend upon others to survive and to make our way in the world; sticking with the group, avoiding conflict, and defaulting to the path of least resistance can be a sensible course of action. If we follow the rules and avoid offense, we keep ourselves in good stead with our social group and can rely on it for help should fate make it necessary to do so. If, as some researchers suggest, we experience social pain—rejection, exclusion, ostracism—in the same way that we experience physical pain, avoiding social pain keeps us strong and safe, which is a powerful motivation to conform.[1] In more circumstances than we care to admit, we use threats and intimidation—including violence—to punish and persuade those who don't conform. And because things often change more quickly than we can know, a safe way to stay out of trouble with the group is to simply do what everyone else is doing.

Yet as my mother implored, refusing to follow the crowd, even when it appears to be a threat to one's own personal survival, is also an important social skill. Sometimes the crowd is headed in the wrong direction. Moreover, without independent thinking, non-conforming choice, and the ability to inspire others to envision change, we would not collectively survive and make progress: prescient vision; heroic action; scientific breakthroughs; innovative applications of science, technology, philosophy, and social science; and inventions in art, architecture, literature, and music all lead to better ways of doing things in private and in public life.

However, the value of non-conformance is often only apparent in retrospect. Steve Jobs, Steve Wozniak, every living Nobel Laureate, and those who have survived genocide, can recount the trials and tribulations of bucking the crowd. Other changes are not just difficult but intensely controversial and violent: the American and French revolutions—and all other armed insurrections; the acts of terror and social and economic disturbance that broke apartheid in South Africa; stem cell research, cloning, and other innovations in the biological sciences. Still other, seemingly benign changes prove to be troublesome until we adapt: the unintended consequences of recent innovations in structuring financial risk; the advances and risks associated with Internet-based exchange; the rise of a new generation that is 2 billon-strong and hungry for change.

Why do we conform in some cases and buck the status quo in others? Of equal importance, how do we know what someone else will do and, hence, our best response? It seems clear that in order to safely navigate life's shoals, we must be able to understand our own motivations as well as those of others.

Motivating

Standard economic and policy models assume that the motivation for all human choice can be attributed to the quest for monetary gain or things that can lead to monetary gain, such as a good reputation or a position of influence. And they fail to consider the full costs of deviating from the status quo. Consumers seek to maximize the value received for a dollar spent, regardless of the impact on relations with others; businesses seek to maximize profit; non-profit organizations and politicians would like to maximize revenues or votes; property owners want to maximize the public services they receive and minimize the taxes they pay; workers seek the highest wage possible for the least amount of effort; managers want to pay the lowest wage for the highest effort.

Yet the evidence for economic optimization as a primary source of motivation is ambiguous. Although the prospect of gain is important in some of the choices we make, we also consistently and pervasively do things with no hope of gain: we donate blood; volunteer our time; work more with no additional pay; exert effort to excel at a craft that is little valued; make anonymous donations; and invest time and money in developing new skills. We even do things that are difficult, painful, costly, or punishing without compensation, like ride in rodeos, bear children, run with the bulls, jump out of airplanes, exercise until it hurts, take an unpopular stand, participate in rebellions and suicide bombings, and volunteer to serve our country in military and civilian engagements. Even more curiously, in some cases, when we are offered money to do something we are doing without pay, we stop doing it or do less of it. You may, for example, be delighted to spontaneously shovel a neighbor's walk after a snowstorm, but wouldn't dream of doing so if your neighbor offered to pay you to provide regular snow-removal services.

If we aren't strictly motivated by money or the absence of pain, and if the prospect of gain can actually reduce our motivation to act, why do we do what we do? Economist Bruno Frey argues that we are motivated by both "extrinsic" factors such as gains, losses, or sanctions and by inner satisfaction or "intrinsic" factors. Unlike extrinsic motivation, intrinsic motivation can be quashed or "crowded out" by monetary incentives or threatening actions. To see how this works, let's go back to shoveling snow.

It is a bright crisp day. Having shoveled your walk, you are feeling invigorated. Delighted by the day and the exercise, you decide to shovel your neighbor's walk as well. As you are whistling and mindlessly scooping the snow onto the boulevard, content with all and sundry, your neighbor comes out, surveys the results achieved, and suggests that you make some changes in the way you are shoveling. He offers to give you a beer when you finish and goes back indoors, where he watches you with keen interest. Although you have never been known to shy away from a beer or an audience, instead of whistling while you shovel, enjoying the attention and anticipating a well-earned reward, you inexplicably find yourself feeling trapped, grinding your teeth, thinking unkind thoughts about your neighbor, and longing to break away.

What accounts for your change of mind with respect to this task and your view of your neighbor? Neither the task nor the environment have changed: It is still a beautiful day and the benefits of exercise and doing something useful in the neighborhood are undiminished. Moreover, you now have an audience and the prospect of a nice cold beer when you finish. Yet it no longer feels the same, and your motivation to complete the project is sharply curtailed no matter how much you "reason" with yourself. The change that has occurred is in your mind.

Mind Reading

It is cliché but nonetheless true that we are inescapably social creatures: The boundaries between who we are uniquely and those with whom we are interacting are tenuous and easily pierced. "Them" is often us: Thinking, choice, and action are influenced by the actual, imagined, or implied presence of others. In social interaction, our minds are viral, and they are contagious. Think of the last time you were feeling cheerful and spry until you had lunch with an angry, anxious, or depressed friend. Or perhaps you have felt soothed and pacific in the presence of someone who was tranquil, calm, and accepting. Had you been observed as part of a social psychology experiment in either of these circumstances, researchers would note changes in your facial expressions, posture, and body movements; pulse and heart rates; release of stress hormones; your perception of your own state of mind; your attitudes; and so on.

We are all mind-readers, and the minds of others are always involved when we think and choose. The ability to understand social signals and to perceive and transmit mental desires and beliefs is a quiet cornerstone of our intelligence and functionality. It begins to develop before the age of one, continues to strengthen throughout our lives, and is believed to be an important element in learning and knowledge production. What is involved in forming a social mind? First, we must in some fashion know our own minds. Second, we must be able to intuit the minds of others. Finally, we must be able to reason with some modicum of accuracy about what is in our minds, what we think may be in the minds of others, and to calculate how the minds of others ought to affect our plans and actions (see Figure 6.1).

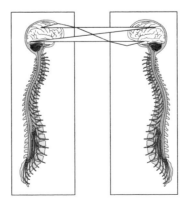

Figure 6.1 Mind Reading

Knowing Our Own Minds

The first thing that happens in any social interaction is that there is some type of trigger that sets neurobiological signaling in motion. In most cases, we do not consciously perceive this trigger or directly associate it with a change of mind. Hence, to know our own minds, we must first experience them and then consciously craft an explanation for what we are experiencing.

In our snow-shoveling example, the trigger may be the appearance of your neighbor. Hearing the door open, perhaps you open your stance, turn to greet your neighbor, and smile warmly, only to see him hunched-up and grimacing in the doorway. Your hearty "hello" appears to be reciprocated by a more restrained, and somewhat hostile, response.

In a moment, you have taken in your neighbor's facial expression, body posture, tone of voice, and his words. Neurobiological signaling commences before you are fully aware of your state of mind, and you begin to experience sensations, feelings, emotions, and memories of related experience. Thoughts, of which you are only vaguely aware, bubble up, begin to tumble around, and trigger more signaling.

Data suggests that while our brains exhibit ongoing spontaneous "thinking," self-awareness is rather sketchy and fleeting.[2] Moreover, there is competition between motivations to attend to self-related versus goal-related activities. Signaling in a disparate set of brain regions synchronizes to influence how much we pay attention to different aspects of ourselves. When triggers are particularly meaningful, there is more activation in these areas, but when they are less meaningful or could interfere with performing even more meaningful tasks, activity is attenuated.

How we think about what happens in social interaction, meaningfulness, and motivation is largely determined by prior learning and experience. This, in turn, has shaped the interactions among what Gerald Edelman has called our "value systems," or the neurotransmitters that excite and inhibit neurobiological signaling in our sensory and brain systems, including our emotional systems.

The roles of two prominent neurotransmitters illustrate their importance in understanding motivation. Experiencing pleasure, which is associated with the release of dopamine, reinforces learning and satisfaction and facilitates higher-level reasoning. Dopamine is involved in signaling across sensory and brain systems associated with attention, memory, problem-solving, and movement. The release of dopamine is stimulated by things, which through training and experience, become associated with pleasure, such as the smell of a good cup of coffee, food, sex, indicators of social approval such as praise or a pat on the back, money, or some types of drugs.

On the other side of the spectrum, excitement and threat stimulate the release of stress-related neurotransmitters, such as epinephrine, which is also known as adrenaline, and cortisol. These neurotransmitters boost the flow of oxygen and glucose to the brain and muscles and are associated with hyper-arousal and freezing, fighting, or fleeing in the face of threat. Abnormal levels of stress-related neurotransmitters interfere with our ability to use higher-level reasoning functions: You may have noticed this effect the last time you were "overcome" by excitement or "panic-stricken."

Lawrence Barsalou and his colleagues argue that a good deal of what we learn and experience becomes "embodied" in facial expressions, postures, gestures, and so on.[3] These body states then become associated with specific states of mind that include sensations, emotions, memory, and thoughts. Social interaction can trigger body states, and body states can affect how we feel and what we think, which in turn, affects motivation and performance. For example, there is substantial experimental evidence that when we interact, we mimic each others' expressions, speech patterns, gestures, and emotional tone. When we are smiling, we think funny things are funnier than when we are frowning; when we adopt an upright posture, we feel more confident; when we engage in approach movements, such as pulling something toward us, our attitude is more positive than when we engage in avoidance movements, such as pushing something away from us.

A key aspect of how we know our own mind and generate motivation is our tendency to reason by association and to be unduly influenced by past experience, which leads us to assume that what takes place in a current interaction is directed at us personally, that it will occur in all similar situations, and that the experience will persist over time. As Bruno Frey points out, motivation is subject to what economists call "spill-over" effects—that is, the effects of an action spread beyond the immediate situation, spilling over into other areas. For example, in our snow-shoveling example, your experience with your neighbor may not only reduce your motivation to complete the task at hand, but you may also find yourself unwilling to undertake any other work on his behalf, such as raking leaves or trimming a hedge. Moreover, it may put you off neighborly assistance all together, and you may find yourself reluctant to help anyone in your neighborhood.

However, all is not lost: We are not entirely subject to subconscious neurobiological associations nor permanently haunted by training and past experience. There is also strong evidence that we are able to consciously engage systems in the prefrontal cortex that are involved in higher-level reasoning to moderate signaling in the emotional systems. Dubbed "reappraisal" by psychologists, or giving someone or something the "benefit of the doubt" in folk wisdom, this activity involves consciously and dispassionately reappraising situations, which can counter-balance the signaling associated with feelings and emotions. In our snow-shoveling example, it may be the case that your neighbor is elderly, hard of hearing, often in pain, and suffering from osteoporosis: He is fond of you and appreciates your help, but because of his physical ailments, the way he conveys his feelings is distorted.

Perhaps it has occurred to you that there is a fine line between giving someone the benefit of the doubt and bamboozling ourselves. Or that our tendency to reason by neurobiological association may

mislead us, causing us to connect past experience with a novel interaction that is only superficially equivalent. This would all be solved if
we could read each others' minds—it turns out that in many respects
we can.

Knowing the Minds of Others

An important implication of being social creatures is that we survive by virtue of our ability to quickly and accurately intuit the motivations, feelings, beliefs, and prospective actions of others. In short,
we must have the capacity to "mentalize" or to model each others'
minds, intentions, and limitations. Our capacity to do so, which begins
to develop in early childhood, is well-established. Less clear is how it
is that we are able to do so, individual differences in performance, and
ways in which this capacity may be biased or disrupted.[4]

One line of research suggests that we have a system of "mirror
neurons" that allow us to simulate and mimic the states of others. This,
in turn, allows us to simulate the inner states of the people with whom
we are interacting—to "get inside their head"—and thereby estimate
their intentions and respond accordingly. In "monkey see, monkey do"
fashion, when we imagine, see, smell, hear, or in some cases, touch the
actions or emotional states of others, it triggers the same neurobiological activity that we would experience if we were engaged in the iden-
tical action or emotional state. When we watch someone throw a ball,
we experience the same pattern of neurobiological activity that we
would if we were to throw a ball ourselves. Similarly, when we see
someone suffering or touch someone's tears, we literally experience
sadness and pain.

As you may suspect, if our ability to understand others and their
intentions is based on a system of mirror neurons, this suggests that all
other things being equal, a person with extensive, wide-ranging experience and broadly developed skills is probably better prepared to
accurately understand others' intentions than someone with less experience or skill. Perhaps you have had the pleasure of watching a child

mimic the actions or attitudes of others—animate or inanimate—and then learn through reinforcement to perform these actions in an appropriate context. The data suggest that this process does not end with childhood: It appears that we continue to build and expand our repertoire of mental models throughout our lives—to develop the neurobiological connections that literally produce a feel for people and situations—through mimicry, simulation, and inference.

The larger our repertoire of mental models, the more accurately we can understand others and predict their intentions. Conversely, in those situations when we observe ourselves or others looking on helplessly or exhibiting "cluelessness," assuming it does not reflect disease or disorder, it likely reflects a dearth of similar training, experience, or perhaps capacity, rather than a motivational deficit or a failure of will. Consider, for example, the political and economic transition in Iraq. Sanctions, military force, detailed plans, "roadmaps," technical assistance, cajoling, side-payments, and sanctions have all failed to induce transformation to a democratic, secular, market-driven political economy. From a neurobiological perspective, the core problem in this situation may not be the political will of Iraqis, but a misalignment between and among the Iraqis' mental models of social order, and those of the Bush Administration, the U.S. Congress, and assorted onlookers.

The best way to improve social understanding might be to acquire relevant experience of each others' realities, either directly or through simulation, and thereby lay down the neurobiological tracks necessary to understand each other and accurately assess each others' intentions. This is a two-way street, requiring each party to live in the others' reality. Desegregation, foreign exchange programs, "embedding" journalists in military units, and creating "bull pens" and flat organizations in which managers and line staff work together, are all examples of ways in which we may plumb each other's realities and develop broader mental repertoires.

An alternative approach is to identify an analogous situation that will trigger a signaling pattern that is comparable to what one would experience in a particular situation. Perhaps a pilot and a sailor can understand each other's mental model of navigation by associating wing trim and sail trim; a person who has ridden a roller coaster may be able to mentally approximate a sky diver's experience of free-fall; Americans may understand Jihadists if they reflect on their own youthful experience seeking adventure and release from restrictive social orders; anyone who has ever subordinated their own interests or needs to those of another may be able to understand the mind of a suicide bomber.

Our brains and bodies model the actions of others in much the same way that they model our own actions. As Vittorio Gallese observes, there can be no other persons independent of us.[5] Change begins with the way we think and choose; to change our minds or those of others, we must change brains, bodies, and environments.

Changing Minds

Philosophers—and certain intrepid neuroscientists—have a long tradition of wrestling with the idea of human existence. The "mind-body" problem, as this endeavor is called, has to do with explaining the relationship between mental states and body states in order to speculate about how they influence each other. Although a philosopher colleague is quick to remind me that all the sciences—physical and social—are descended from philosophy, I for one am willing to admit that many of the rest of us are a somewhat ruder sort who easily tire in existential debates. Even ruder still are those of us who prefer to mix-it-up in the world of problems that human existence has wrought. In this world, as I have argued in Chapters 4, "Thinking in the Wild," and 5, "Feeling Our Way," when it comes to how we think and choose, our best evidence suggests that the mind-body problem is a mind-body-environment problem. If we wish to understand our own intentions, the intentions of others, and arrive at our best response, our challenge is to explain how our experience in all three states interacts to affect thinking and choice: our own and others.

When we begin to think about change, further complications en-sue. In order to achieve change, we have to simultaneously change our actions as well as our minds, bodies, and environment (see Figure 6.2). If we would like to change from being landlubbers to sailors, we must begin to act like sailors; deck shoes and salty language will not take us safely down river. We must step off the dock into a boat, rig it properly, hoist the sails, find the wind, set our course, and venture forth. We can go to sailing school, study sailing, and learn some sailing instructions and routines such as navigational rules, work with rigging, and experi-ment with the affects of airflow on model sails set in particular config-urations. But we will not become sailors until we have retrained our bodies and brains, which requires acquiring experience sailing a boat under a wide range of conditions: fair and foul weather, high and low tides, heavy and light traffic, with more- and less-capable crews, and so on. Then, and only then, will we have created the mind-body-environ-ment habits of being that distinguish us from landlubbers.

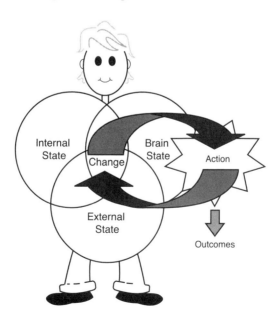

Figure 6.2   Intuitive Change

Changing would be a relatively simple exercise in individual choice, except for the fact that we live and work in social groups in particular environments that may or may not be conducive to the changes we wish to or ought to make. Imagine how much more difficult it is to think about and choose to be a sailor if those with whom you regularly interact are landlubbers who don't like sailors, or if there are severe rules and sanctions that prohibit someone like you from sailing. Or maybe you live in a desert, far from water. Could you even imagine sailing or aspire to be a sailor in these circumstances?

Let's say that you have a hard-wired pre-disposition to be an accomplished sailor. Perhaps you are descended from a long line of sailors; or your imagination has been fired by stories or images about sailing. In either case, you yearn to sail. If sailing is socially unacceptable in your group, to satisfy this yearning, you must strike out on your own, find a group where it is acceptable for you to sail, and bear the costs of doing so. If you live in a desert, it must be physically possible to safely travel to a place with water, and you must be able to finance the cost of your travels. You have the motivation to sail; now you must find ways to mitigate the risks and finance the costs of pursuing this ambition.

Although changing ourselves when we want to change is difficult in the best circumstances, changing an entire social order when some do not wish to do so is an even greater challenge. Well-intended, large-scale social change efforts, such as organizational change, social revolution, or insurgencies, fail more often than they succeed. By now, it should be easy to see why large-scale change is so unlikely: To change results, one must change patterns of action. To change patterns of action, one must change many minds and bodies, who in turn are embedded in contexts that include the physical conditions or state of nature in which they live, their everyday rules of the game, and the relationships and networks that make up their social world.[6]

As distinct from the esoteric world of metaphysics, the primary challenge in the more pragmatic world of human existence is to

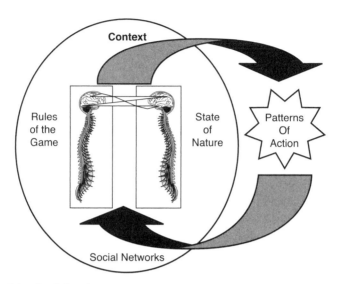

Figure 6.3   Social order

comprehend and adapt to challenges that threaten our continued survival. Adaptation requires change, and although we are wired in such a way that we have the potential to accurately comprehend the challenges before us and make adaptive change, this potential is constrained by our experience. With almost seven billion people in the world today living in many different contexts, there are profound differences among us. Yet our continued survival requires that we craft a common context in those areas that are most closely associated with mutual survival: The long war before us is not with each other, but with ourselves. Can we use what we are learning about how we really think and choose to make more secure choices in the years ahead?

7

Brightening the Twinkle of Our Faded Star

"Don't be stupid."
—*My father, who I hope rests in peace despite my many errors.*

If the state of research today in the neurosciences demonstrates anything useful at all for today's policy makers and others who are concerned with governing societies of minds, it is that following my father's advice is rather difficult—a hit-or-miss proposition at best. It appears that we think and choose quite differently than standard economic and public policy models suggest. Rather than being dispassionate optimization machines with stable preferences and an objective knowledge base (that we update, following Bayes' rule), we are highly advanced but biased sensory systems that adapt intuitively to a physical and social context that is partly real and partly imagined. Our stock of knowledge is a pattern of neurobiological connections that integrates sensations, emotions, and past training and experience; our actions spring from neuronal signaling triggered by our perception of our experience in our environment, which generates associations between what we perceive to be going on around us and our experiences in past interactions in similar circumstances.

Many of our choices are automatic rather than the product of calculation: "thinking" occurs after a choice has been made. Although we have the capacity to acquire and use logic tools to reduce bias in thinking and choice, to the extent that we put these tools to use, we often override them when we face a meaningful threat—in some instances to good effect—and we side-step danger. In other cases, we are less adept. As I write, mania and panic in the financial markets is a cogent reminder of this propensity. In short, our powers of reason can fail us when they are most needed.

With threats of one sort or another vying for our attention, what can we do to minimize this potentially self-destructive state of affairs? In recent years, the most prominent silver bullet to penetrate policy analysis is game theory—in fact, few fields have escaped its pervasive influence. As you may know, game theory is an analytical approach to understanding strategic choice, which is the type of choice that arises whenever we need to figure out what others may do to select our own best course of action. Because many of the choices we make involve strategic interaction with others, game theory is an appealing approach if you are motivated by my father's imperative. This is particularly true in matters involving security.

However, as is the case with many analytical tools, the benefits of game theory are often misunderstood: The technique has been too-hastily applied to complex policy problems that are poorly described, problems have been over-simplified to fit the technique, and the results of these misfit analyses have been too naively accepted and interpreted.

Consider, for example, the problem that confronted occupants of the World Trade Center on 9/11 who could not safely jump to the ground from the floor they were on when the attacks occurred. Should they stay in their offices, as they were urged to do, or leave the building? If they decided to leave the building, should they use the elevator or the stairs? If they used the stairs, which stairwell should they use? The best answer to these questions depends upon what they knew, what other people knew, the actions available to them, the actions taken by others, and the potential outcomes of action.

Yet the 9/11 exit problem is very difficult to model, particularly if you are in the midst of it. You are not sure what is going on, and you cannot obtain additional information—you know that there is a crisis, but you do not know the precise nature of the crisis, the full extent of the crisis, or how long it will last. What should you do? If you know that those who are urging you to stay know with certainty what is going on and can guarantee your safety, it would be wise to follow their advice. On the other hand, if they have bad information or an inadequate rescue operation, it might be wiser still to ignore their advice. With very limited information, you must estimate the probability of each of these potential scenarios and bet your life on the best course of action.

If you decide to leave, your choice of exit is complicated by several additional factors. What is the probability that the elevators will continue to work throughout the crisis and that you can avoid getting stuck? What is the probability that the stairwells are clear, and which one is most likely to remain clear? What is the probability that the exit you choose to use will be so congested that you will not get out in time or that you will be hurt or perhaps trampled to death in the process? Let's add one more complication. Your officemate is paraplegic: Should you stay with him or go for help, as he is urging you to do? If you go for help, what is the probability that you can get help to him in time? If you leave him, and you survive but he perishes, can you live with this result?

Game theoretic techniques can help us understand the questions, risks, and sources of uncertainty in strategic situations. However, they may not help us usefully model the challenges we face, and they most definitely cannot provide us with an unambiguous solution.

Ariel Rubinstein, an adroit and exceedingly thoughtful game theorist who has extended John Nash's Nobel Prize-winning work, has been thinking about human rationality for a long time. Arguing that orthodox economic models are unrealistic and dogmatic, he suggests that the real challenge is to change the thinking of those who think about choice. Although interested in behavioral economics and "neuroeconomics"—an emerging sub-discipline that seeks to understand the brain activity associated with economic decision making—Rubinstein is critical of the research agenda, the way research is being performed, and the results that are being reported. He believes that there is a tendency among researchers to ask uninteresting questions and to reach conclusions without sufficient evidence. He makes the very sensible suggestion that economists use data about the human mind to develop richer models of bounded rationality that make more realistic assumptions about human choice.[1]

Neuroscience research is in its infancy: There is far more that we don't know about how we think and choose than we know. As a fellow social scientist and an irrepressible meddler in human affairs, I am as eager as Ariel Rubinstein to discover valid and reliable data that can help analysts develop better models of thinking and choice. But what type of data do we need? And until the course of normal science wends its way to more nearly valid and reliable results, how can we better inform our intuition about how we should proceed in the meantime?

Rethinking Difficult Questions

The received wisdom among many in the United States is that the terrorist attacks on September 11, 2001 changed the world and changed our lives forever. Although this is a useful rhetorical device to get people with busy brains to pay attention to what one is about to say, there is really very little evidence that this is so. Changes in the global political economy were well in the works long before 9/11: The emerging economies have been growing faster than the developed economies for 25 years, and rapid technological diffusion has increased awareness, interaction, and capabilities. Both factors have fueled geo-political rivalries and dissidence for some time now. And some things never change: Radical extremism, violent conflict, and economic rivalry are consistent themes in world history and up-ticks in modern trends were clearly evident even before Samuel Huntington's widely-read 1996 treatise on the clash of civilizations.[2]

Scholars who study conflict tell us that there are three things that are closely associated with conflict and war: ideological differences including religious differences, economic disparity, and being too close to each other. Despite detailed knowledge about past events and many modern analytical tools, they cannot tell us with certainty when these differences, which are always present to some degree, will become so severe that they erupt in conflict, how they will erupt, what we should do to prevent them, or how best to address them when we are in the thick of it.

Given what we are learning about how we think and choose, it is probably naive to expect scholarship to answer fundamental strategic security questions and deliver good strategic advice. In fact, many would agree with prominent political economist Elinor Ostrom's argument that given the diversity of human life, there are no panaceas or blueprints for governing human interaction.[3] Useful strategic advice requires a detailed understanding of social interaction on the ground that cannot be gleaned from secondary sources or high level estimates, change is too frequent, and the challenges we confront are too different to be represented by a single formal model or even a small class of models. Scholarship and formal modeling can help us understand our questions and use logic tools to augment our intuition, but when push comes to shove, we are the deciders with respect to our own survival; we must both develop our reasoning skills and acquire experience in the world interacting with each other to better develop our intuition.

Rather than trying to boil the scholarly ocean, let's take a look at how a few very experienced people think about the security challenges that confront us in the near term.

How Shall We Defend Ourselves?

As a former Director of the U.S. Central Intelligence Agency, R. James Woolsey is a man who has a deep understanding of the threats we face in the world today. Although no one gets the top job at the CIA without a good resume, Jim's extensive experience gives the moniker "multi-faceted" new meaning: He has held Presidential appointments in four administrations, including two under Democratic Presidents and two under Republicans, been a delegate or ambassador to a number of international arms control negotiations, and served in the military. He also has extensive experience outside the government, including 22 years practicing law as a corporate attorney and five years as a partner in the major international consulting firm Booz Allen Hamilton. In addition, he has held a number of directorships on corporate and civic boards. No less sterling than his experience, Woolsey's education includes a BA from Stanford University, an MA from Oxford, where he was a Rhodes Scholar, and an L.LB from Yale Law School.

Today, Woolsey is a venture partner with VantagePoint in Silicon Valley and a Senior Executive Advisor with Booz Allen Hamilton. He is a frequent and sometimes controversial contributor to public debates on foreign affairs, defense, and intelligence. But his real passions are energy security, climate change, and infrastructure—all in equal measure. In Woolsey's view, we won't be secure until we eliminate our dependency on oil, which he believes is an important source of finance for terrorism; halt our fuel-based contributions to climate change; and use technology to restructure our lives away from large, centralized factory-like settings toward what he calls a "Jeffersonian" classically liberal political economy—more self-reliant individuals living and working in communities linked by distributed infrastructure.

Woolsey's approach to strategic defense has two tightly integrated prongs: 1) shift the primary source of energy from oil to alternative fuels, including electricity; 2) make it more difficult and more expensive to attack human and critical infrastructure targets, and less disruptive should a catastrophic event occur, including both terrorist attacks and natural disasters or pandemic. His two-pronged approach contains many virtuous circles. A few critical targets are now provided by some components of the electricity grid, or by large highly interdependent urban areas, which are more attractive to a terrorist and less difficult to disrupt or destroy than many small targets. Large targets, whether hit by planned attacks or by natural disasters, translate into large impacts and massive disruption. But if we live and work in communities supported by distributed communications and electricity networks, we are not only less-attractive targets that are more difficult to hit, the system-wide impact of catastrophe of one or a few catastrophic events would be less disruptive. We can move in these directions while we use less energy, reduce our dependence on oil, reduce petroleum-finance for terror, and lower CO_2 emissions.

The lynch-pin in Woolsey's defensive strategy is a focus on affordable distributed renewable sources of energy. Putting on his venture capital hat, he has three criteria for ideal investment areas in energy (although some excellent investments will not score on all points): 1) The alternative will reduce CO_2 emissions; 2) it requires, at most, only very modest investment in infrastructure to produce, distribute, and consume; 3) it makes our energy systems less vulnerable to terrorist attacks. At present, given existing technologies and infrastructures, he is particularly keen on investments in distributed energy from renewable sources—such as photovoltaics, batteries, small-scale wind, innovative feedstocks (cellulose, algae, waste, and so on) for liquid fuels, and plug-in hybrid and electric vehicles.

In addition to his investment interests, he has nine very specific proposals to contend with our current security and climate change challenges, as follows:

1. Improve the energy efficiency of buildings.
2. Increase the use of combined heat and power.
3. Create long-term incentives for small-scale (single building-based) distributed generation of electricity and heating/cooling.

4. Decouple revenue from earnings for electric utilities to encourage conservation and investment in grid modernization.

5. Give steady and long-term encouragement to the deployment of renewable electricity generation for the grid from wind, solar, hydro, and geothermal.

6. Vigorously develop carbon capture and sequestration for coalfired power plants.

7. Provide tax incentives for the purchase of plug-in hybrid gasoline-electric vehicles.

8. Mandate a rapid transition to flexible fuel vehicles.

9. Provide incentives for the production of renewable fuels and specialty chemicals from cellulosic biomass, algae, and other such feedstocks; give special attention to the desirability of using waste products as a feedstock, particularly where methane is thereby reduced.

Leveraging long experience and solid training, Woolsey provides us with a well-informed, intuitive approach to thinking about domestic security in today's changing geo-political realities that can be generalized and extended to address rivalries over other strategic resources such as finance, minerals and metals, biodiversity, water, and so on. Yet in strategic games, sometimes the best defense is a good offense. So let's turn from defensive to offensive strategy.

What Offensive Actions Should We Take?

"In the post-September 11 world, irregular warfare has emerged as the dominant form of warfare confronting the United States, its allies, and its partners; accordingly, guidance must account for distributed, long-duration operations, including unconventional warfare, foreign internal defense, counterterrorism, counterinsurgency, and stabilization and reconstruction operations."

—.S. Quadrennial Defense Review Report, February 6, 2006

"We need to be prepared to fight a different war. This is another type of war, new in its intensity, ancient in its origin, war by guerilla, subversives, insurgents, assassins; war by ambush instead of combat, by infiltration instead of aggression, seeking victory by eroding and exhausting the enemy instead of engaging him. It requires, in those situations where we encounter it, a whole new strategy, a wholly different kind of force, and therefore, a new and wholly different kind of military training."

—*President John F. Kennedy, 1962 U.S. Military Academy Commencement Address*

Warfare is an emotionally charged subject—perhaps you are even now recoiling as you read. Yet it is a common choice, much as we may regret it, used by both liberals and conservatives to protect or extend deeply felt values and interests. Waging war is something that most western societies leave to military professionals who live and work in a separate world of their own. However, without exposure to military training and experience, it is exceedingly difficult to think about warfare, publicly debate it, and make good choices.

With the prose of a politician and the experience of an officer in World War II, President Kennedy described the need to rethink warfare. This "different war" as he put it, or the more confounding "irregular warfare" as it is called today, is different with respect to conventional warfare. World War II is a good example of conventional warfare: state against state, prosecuted by professionally trained military forces under government control with the aim of strengthening one state and its government at the expense of another. Conventional warfare is a struggle to control territory and resources and to subjugate a population to the will of the prevailing state.

By contrast, irregular warfare is what we prosecuted in the Cold War, what we experienced in the United States on 9/11, and what our allies, troops, and advisors are experiencing in Iraq, Afghanistan, and Pakistan: a struggle among state and non-state groups to "win the hearts and minds" of groups of people whose support is important in a struggle for political and economic influence. "Warriors," who are quite different from each other and often difficult to discern, do not have common rules of engagement, and they rarely play by the same rules. They seek to erode their rivals' power and influence and to undermine their will to continue to compete. Irregular warfare is a complex mix of offensive and defensive operations that meet humanitarian needs, restore order, and stabilize social life, which can include conventional tactics: Culture, history, local circumstances, information, communications, psychology, law enforcement, community development and a keen understanding of the dynamics of social change are as important and perhaps more important than the use of force.[4]

Forty-six years later, we are still struggling to rise to President Kennedy's challenge to think about and conduct ourselves differently in conducting offensive security operations that protect U.S. interests. Brigadier General Patrick Donahue and Lieutenant Colonel Michael Fenzel are two experienced U.S. Army officers who have been on the forefront of meeting this challenge. Despite considerable experience and extensive education—BG Donahue holds a BS from the U.S. Military Academy, an MPA from Harvard University, and an MS in National Security Studies from the U.S. Army War College; and LTC Fenzel holds a BA from Johns Hopkins and two masters degrees in national security studies from Harvard University and the U.S. Naval War College—the nature of how humans think and choose creates social change dynamics that demand that they feel their way intuitively in response to the conditions they find on the ground.

In a recent article for *Military Review*, BG Donahue and LTC Fenzel describe their experience conducting modern irregular warfare in a country weakened by 25 years of conflict that had become a hotbed of terrorist activity.[5] In June 2005, BG Donahue and deputy commander LTC Fenzel took command of the 1st Brigade of the 82nd Airborne Division, assuming responsibility for supporting counter-insurgency operations in 10 provinces in a mountainous region in Afghanistan roughly the size of North Carolina; 5,000 soldiers, sailors, airmen, and marines; and eight provincial reconstruction teams. In addition to working with the Afghan government, the Afghan National Army, and local police, their mission also required close cooperation with Special Operations Forces and other U.S. government agencies operating in the area.

As BG Donahue and LTC Fenzel describe it, their mission goals were to stabilize the area; reduce the influence of rivals of the government of Afghanistan, which included Taliban, Al-Qaeda, Gulbaddin, and Hizb-i Islami groups; protect the people; and work with Afghanis to build their capacity to create a secure, self-governing political economy. In short, their aim was not to kill and capture rival groups but to give the people in the area compelling reasons to support the Afghan government rather than succumb to the incendiary religious appeals, terrorism, intimidation, and other forms of violence fomented by rivals.

Those of you who have had the experience of working with groups with a legacy of conflict, poverty, inadequate infrastructure, corruption, smuggling, drug and arms trafficking, and refugee migration will understand the enormity of the challenge confronted by this Combined Task Force. Functioning a bit like armed anthropologists, six principles guided their operations, as follows:

1. Make every operation a combined operation with Afghan counterparts.

2. Always seek mass effects, partnering with the Afghanis to identify missions of mutual interest.

3. Make an understanding of local traditions and the Afghan people a significant part of the operations planning process.

4. Seek operational interoperability with military forces on the border.

5. Treat Afghans with respect and display discipline at all times.

6. Apply combat power, civil-military expertise, and information operations simultaneously.

Another important principle emerged from their experience on the ground: to engage community elders and the community itself in planning reconstruction and stabilization activities, and to make sure that they have a stake in completing and protecting the project over the long haul. In other words, troops involved in irregular warfare become deeply involved in community development. Part soldier, part technical advisor, and part public works specialist, today's troops have a very complex and exceedingly difficult job that they must learn by doing. Unfortunately, political and economic development is a very idiosyncratic process and there is a great deal that we do not know about how it occurs. However we do know from well-researched field experiments and we can surmise from the emerging social neuroscience literature that no matter how well intended or carefully planned, development is not something that one can do to someone or for someone. To achieve sustainable results, the social context has to change, which means that enough people in a community must change their minds, their social networks, and the rules of the game. In other words, those who are the object of development must do it their own way in their own time. Outsiders can help, but they cannot control the means or the process.

Perhaps the most effective principles that guide BG Donahue's and LTC Fenzel's approach to irregular warfare are not listed in their article: a genuine humility about their work; and a commitment to learning, sharing their experience, and critically examining options including the decision to attempt to change others' hearts and minds, no matter how well-intended.

It has no doubt occurred to you that security—whether defensive or offensive—is expensive, which suggests a third set of difficult questions.

Figure 7.1   U.S. and Afghan military officers meeting with local police and elders in Chapadara, Kunar province

How Should We Protect Our Means to Finance Action?

Although it may be the case that money can't buy us love, it is sure a big help when it comes to security. Because money does not grow in ATMs, and printing too much of it is counter-productive, we need a strong financial system that we can rely on to safely and prudently transfer funds from those with surplus to those who can invest them in ways that will produce economic growth and generate revenues that can be invested to protect the public interest. Moreover, as the Emperors' Club clients were recently reminded, monitoring financial flows is one way to identify and prosecute a full spectrum of illegal and potentially threatening activity, from prostitution to terrorism, which is good defensive and offensive security strategy.

Finance, like warfare, is a rather esoteric subject that many of us leave to specialists, who communicate in mind-numbing jargon and use mind-blowing techniques to assess and structure transactions that coalesce in complex systemic interactions. Yet a well-functioning financial system is the backbone of an economy and crucial to competitiveness.

In addition to facilitating the allocation of funds among alternative uses, a financial system also regulates the humans and the tools that are involved in the process. Markets are a wonderful mechanism for allocating investment; however, price bubbles are ubiquitous, which in turn provides the perfect set-up for manias, panics, and crashes.[6] Evidence from neuroscience helps to explain why this is so: Our risk estimates are systematically biased. When we experience a threat, such as falling prices, our ability to regulate our emotional systems is easily compromised; one person's experience is contagious, rapidly leading to mass effects.

The bottom line is that financial markets cannot function effectively without sensible regulation and prudent supervision. The question at any given moment in time is how to strike the right balance between protecting investors and the financial system, the cost of protection, and the competitiveness of the system with respect to other financial systems. After all, financial assets are even more mobile than people and easily move to the least restrictive environment.

Over a long career in government service, consulting, and academia, Robert Glauber has made it his mission to demystify finance and keep intelligent financial regulation on the public agenda. An intrepid intellectual with Socratic style, Glauber has made it a habit to bring business, law, and public policy thinking to bear on these issues, even venturing to bring Harvard students from all three schools together in the same seminar. Recently retired as Chairman and CEO of the National Association of Securities Dealers, Glauber has served as Under Secretary of the Treasury for Finance, Executive Director of the Brady Commission, and Professor of Finance at the Harvard Business School. In addition to serving as an Adjunct in the Kennedy School, he has also served as a Visiting Professor at Harvard Law School. And, he holds an AB and DBA from Harvard University.

Glauber is focusing his attention these days on capital market regulation. Having worked on the October 1987 stock market crash, regulatory overhaul and recapitalization of the savings and loan industry,

regulatory reform in commercial banking, and changes to the procedures for auctioning Treasury securities, he is no stranger to financial
markets infected by what Nobel Laureate John Maynerd Keynes
called "animal spirits." As the recent crisis in U.S. financial markets
demonstrates, we have for too long neglected regulation of counterparty risk and derivatives, issues that affect both capital market and
banking supervision. As a member of the Committee on Capital Markets Regulation—an independent, bi-partisan committee of 22 corporate and finance leaders from investment, business, finance, law,
accounting, and academic communities—Glauber points to the need
for a number of reforms.

1. Regulatory process reforms that would require the use of more
    risk-based processes, and that are focused explicitly on the costs
    and benefits of regulation; principles-based rules that guide
    rather than prescribe behavior; better coordination among reg-
    ulatory authorities.

2. Private and public enforcement reforms that would provide
    greater clarity about liabilities that are subject to private litiga-
    tion; make criminal enforcement a last resort reserved solely for
    companies that have become criminal enterprises; prevent the
    failure of another major audit firm.

3. Shareholder rights reforms that would give shareholders the
    right to approve poison-pills in companies with staggered
    boards; majority rather than plurality voting rules; shareholder
    access to the director nominating process; the right to adopt al-
    ternative dispute resolution processes as an alternative to tradi-
    tional litigation.

4. No statutory changes to the Sarbanes-Oxley Act but changes to
    the implementation of Section 404 that would deliver the same
    benefits while reducing the cost of compliance.

And, Glauber adds, we need to reduce the national debt.

The Capital Markets Committee was organized to explore issues related to maintaining and improving the competitiveness of U.S. capital markets, which like many other sectors of American life is increasingly buffeted by changes among societies in a world that we do not, never have, and cannot control. We cannot be secure if we are not competitive. However, competitiveness, which includes knowing when to cooperate and with whom, depends not only upon our strategic savvy but also upon our ability to govern ourselves. Each of the voices you have heard in this chapter is concerned in one way or another with self-governance, so let's turn to this topic as our final stop.

How Shall We Govern Ourselves in the Years Ahead?

Thinking about this problem, I am beset by the memory of a brightly colored, artificially intelligent plastic bug I recently saw demonstrated in a technology store. The bug was programmed to move forward until it hit an obstacle, back up slightly, and then experiment by moving either right or left until it could continue unimpeded. This mapping served it rather well, with only occasional bouts of signaling-induced confusion until it came to the edge of the counter where, unimpeded, it marched naively into the void and crashed to the floor.

Like artificially intelligent creatures, we function for the most part on auto-pilot, following routine maps that guide us in our forward march: Many of us don't experiment with a novel direction until we are impeded or crash. We are also error-prone in much the same way: Signaling runs amok, and we go off-map. But unlike artificially intelligent creatures, we are wired for survival. We have many more sensing capabilities and infinitely more maps. We live in environments that are much more complex than a retail store countertop, and most importantly, we can add to and change our maps. But this is small comfort indeed if we fail to use our capacities at the critical moment.

We have been forewarned by numerous data that if we follow our usual map, our forward march at home and abroad is impeded—it may even take us smack into the void. If we wish to survive, let alone "brighten the twinkle of our fading star," as T.S. Eliot put it so beautifully, the trick is to change maps. It will do no good to rely on others to dream up new policies to address our problems because if we do not change our minds, we will neither produce better policies nor recognize them when they are put forth. As a former business partner used to argue, "If your only tool is a hammer, everything looks like a nail."

Because changing maps is a mind-body-environment problem, to do this successfully, we will need to put ourselves in learning mode and change our environment by exposing ourselves to new minds and new experiences. In short, we must venture out with the curiosity and the courage of an explorer and be willing to adjust ourselves and our path to the conditions we find as we travel. The long war ahead—irregular or otherwise—is as much with ourselves as it is with those who threaten the pursuit of peaceful growth and change.

Still, every explorer needs some rules for the road—so here are a few principles derived from what we are learning about how we think and choose:

1. Sustainable growth and change involves changing the way we think and choose, which means acquiring new experience that changes our mental maps. Changing mental maps involves immersing ourselves, suspending judgment, and striving to understand what other people are doing and why they are doing it, from their perspective. Every environment has an existing order with its own internal logic: It may not be an order we are accustomed to or wish to become accustomed to, but it exists for a reason, and it will not easily change. Hence we might be better served when we share history and experience respectfully, experiment, strive for interoperability rather than wholesale reform, and resist employing fruitless control strategies such as

fiat, proselytizing, finger-wagging, sanctions, side-payments, and force.

2. We are complex many-centered (polycentric) sensory systems. And, as eminent political scientist Vincent Ostrom argues, many of the organizational and governance systems we create—perhaps most—are also polycentric. As distinct from hierarchical systems, polycentric systems have multiple centers of decision making that are formally independent of each other. If you think about it, it makes perfect sense that animals built from distributed networks that are wired for survival are inclined to construct equally resilient political and economic networks. This means the first order of business in exploring any social context is discovering what people value and how they coordinate their activities, which involves identifying key social networks, figuring out how they are organized, and the types of mechanisms they use for social control.[8]

3. Although most thinking and choice is intuitive, unconscious, and directed toward survival, the artful use of logic tools can enhance our adaptive capacity. Sound choices are based on unassailable self-regulation that incorporates sensation, emotion, and logic. Although there are three general approaches to engagement in any situation—compete, cooperate, or avoid—the best approach is the one that fits the situation. Being a one-trick pony—always competing, cooperating, or avoiding or expecting consistency from others—is not an adaptive strategy.

4. Our bodies and brains are primarily engaged in maintaining system balance, which limits our capacity for intensive, unbiased thinking. And that is why it makes good sense to seek and use information from many different individuals and groups, and to make sure that those who have the experience to best sense what is going on in a particular context have the authority and means to act.

5. Although we are wired for survival, the mental maps we rely on to make secure choices are error-prone and biased by our past experience, which means that they might not serve us well in thinking about and managing current and future risks. Perhaps one of the best investments we can make to secure our future is to develop risk management tools that can help us not only attend to and estimate threats, but generate alternative adaptive strategies and make informed trade-offs among them in real time.

6. Our minds are viral and contagious, and we are too-often inclined to follow the crowd even when the crowd is going in the wrong direction. This suggests the need in times of change as well as everyday civil discourse to strike the right balance between "letting it all hang-out" as my generation once put it, and observing the ancient imperative to keep a low profile. Perhaps this balance is most easily accomplished when we seek common ground, work shoulder to shoulder, and make sure that everyone has skin in the game.

As a final offering for the journey ahead, I leave you with the advice of a military analyst, a diplomat, and a philosopher-novelist—each of whom, it seems to me, had a solid grasp of adaptive thinking and choice:

> "Keep strong if possible. In any case, keep cool. Have unlimited patience. Never corner an opponent and always assist him to save his face. Put yourself in his shoes—so as to see things through his eyes. Avoid self-righteousness like the devil—nothing so self-blinding."
>
> —*Basil Henry Liddell Hart, 1960*

> "The ideal relationship demands a certain slight disequilibrium of forces and a relative autonomy of each term with respect to the other ... The essential thing is for the relationship

not to be a tranquil one; the dialogue between oscillation and immobility is what gives culture life and life form."

—*Octavio Paz, 1969*

"Whatever we may do, excess will always keep its place in the heart of man, in the place where solitude is found. We all carry within us our places of exile, our crimes, and our ravages. But our task is not to unleash them on the world; it is to fight them in ourselves and in others."

—*Albert Camus, 1956*

Safe travels.

References

Adolphs, Ralph. 2006. "What Is Special About Social Cognition?" In Cacioppo, John T., Penny S. Visser, and Cynthia L. Pickett. 2006. *Social Neuroscience: People Thinking About Thinking People*. Cambridge, MA: MIT Press.

Atkinson, Anthony P., Michael S.C. Thomas, and Axel Cleeremans. 2000. "Consciousness: Mapping the Theoretical Landscape." *Trends in Cognitive Sciences*. Vol. 4, No. 10, October, 372–382.

Aurelius, Marcus. 2003. *Meditations*. Translated by Gregory Hays. New York, NY: The Modern Library. Originally published in 1559 and composed in the 170s AD.

Barsalou, Lawrence W., Paula M. Niedenthal, Aron K. Barbey, and Jennifer A. Ruppert. 2003. "Social Embodiment." In Ross, Brian H., ed. 2003. *The Psychology of Learning and Motivation*. New York, NY: Academic Press.

Beer, Jennifer S. 2006. "Orbitalfrontal Cortex and Social Recognition." In Cacioppo, John T., Penny S. Visser, and Cynthia L. Pickett. 2006. *Social Neuroscience: People Thinking About Thinking People*. Cambridge, MA: MIT Press.

Liddle-Hart, B.H. 1960. *Deterrent or Defense*. New York, NY: Frederick A. Praeger, Inc.

_____. 1967. Second Revised Edition. Strategy. New York, NY: Meridian.

Buccino, G., F. Binkofski, G.R. Fink, L. Fadiga, L. Fogassi, V. Gallese, R.J. Seitz, K. Zilles, G. Rizzolatti, and H.J. Freund. 2005. "Action Observation Activates Premotor and Parietal Areas in a

Somatotopic Manner: An fMRI Study." In Cacioppo, John T., and Gary G. Berntson, eds. 2005. *Social Neuroscience*. New York, NY: Psychology Press.

Cacioppo, John, and Gary G. Berntson, eds. 2005. *Social Neuroscience*. New York, NY: Psychology Press.

Cacioppo, John T., Penny S. Visser, and Cynthia L. Pickett. 2006. *Social Neuroscience: People Thinking About Thinking People*. Cambridge, MA: MIT Press.

Camus, Albert. 1951. *The Rebel: An Essay on Man in Revolt*. New York, NY: Vintage Books.

Carr, Laurie, Marco Iacoboni, Marie-Charlotte Dubeau, John C. Mazziotta, and Gian Luigi Lenzi. 2005. "Neural Mechanisms of Empathy in Humans: A Relay from Neural Systems for Imitation to Limbic Areas." In Cacioppo, John T., and Gary G. Berntson, eds. 2005. *Social Neuroscience*. New York, NY: Psychology Press.

Clausewitz, Carl von. 1832. *On War*. In Howard, Michael, and Peter Paret, editors and translators. 1993 [1984]. *Carl Von Clausewitz. On War*. New York, NY: Alfred A. Knopf.

Crick, Francis. 1994. *The Scientific Search for the Soul*. New York, NY: Charles Scribner & Sons.

Curtis, C.P., Jr., and F. Greenslet, eds. 1962. *The Practical Cogitator; or, The Thinker's Anthology*. Boston, MA: Houghton Mifflin.

Damasio, Antonio. 2003. *Looking for Spinoza: Joy, Sorrow, and the Feeling Brain*. New York, NY: Harcourt Press.

_____. 1999. *The Feeling of What Happens: Body and Emotion in the Making of Consciousness*. New York, NY: Harcourt Press.

Davis, Douglas D., and Charles A. Holt. 1993. *Experimental Economics*. Princeton, NJ: Princeton University Press.

Diamond, D.W., and P. Dybvig. 1983. "Bank Runs, Deposit Insurance, and Liquidity." *Journal of Political Economy*. 91, 401–419.

Doidge, Norman. 2007. *The Brain That Changes Itself: Stories of Personal Triumph from the Frontiers of Brain Science*. New York, NY: Penguin.

Donahue, Colonel (P) Patrick, and Lieutenant Colonel Michael Fenzel. 2008. "Combating a Modern Insurgency: Combined Task Force Devil in Afghanistan." *Military Review*. March–April, 25–40.

The Economist. 2006. "Who Do You Think You Are? A Survey of the Brain." December 23.

The Economist. 2006. "Survey of the World Economy." September 19.

Edelman, Gerald M. 2006. *Second Nature: Brain Science and Human Knowledge*. New Haven, CT: Yale University Press.

Firth, Chris. 2007. *Making Up the Mind: How the Brain Creates Our Mental World*. Malden, MA: Blackwell Publishing.

Firth, Christopher D., and Daniel M. Wolpert, eds. 2003. *The Neuroscience of Social Interaction: Decoding, Imitating, and Influencing the Actions of Others*. Oxford, England: Oxford University Press.

Frey, Bruno S. 2004. *Dealing with Terrorism—Stick or Carrot?*. Northampton, MA: Edward Elger Publishing, Inc.

_____. 1997. *Not Just for the Money: An Economic Theory of Personal Motivation*. Northampton, MA: Edward Elger Publishing, Inc.

Galesse, Vittorio. 2003. "The Manifold Nature of Interpersonal Relations: The Quest for a Common Understanding." In Firth, Christopher D., and Daniel M. Wolpert, eds. 2003. *The Neuroscience of Social Interaction: Decoding, Imitating, and Influencing the Actions of Others*. Oxford, England: Oxford University Press.

Galula, David. 1964. *Counterinsurgency Warfare: Theory and Practice*. New York, NY: Frederick A. Praeger Publishers.

Gazzaniga, Michael S. 2005. *The Ethical Brain*. New York, NY: Dana Press.

_____. Editor in Chief. 2004. *The Cognitive Neurosciences III*. Cambridge, MA: MIT Press.

_____. 1998. *The Mind's Past*. Berkeley, CA: University of California Press.

Gazzaniga, Michael S., Richard B. Ivry, and George R. Mangun. 2002. *Cognitive Neuroscience: The Biology of the Mind*. Second Edition. New York, NY: W.W. Norton and Company.

Glimcher, Paul W., Colin F. Camerer, Ernst Fehr, and Russell A. Poldrack, eds. 2008. *Neuroeconomics: Decision Making and the Brain*. Burlington, MA: Academic Press.

Gusnard, Debra A. 2006. "Neural Substrates of Self-Awareness." Cacioppo, John T., Penny S. Visser, and Cynthia L. Pickett. 2006. *Social Neuroscience: People Thinking About Thinking People*. Cambridge, MA: MIT Press.

Haidt, Jonathan. 2001. "The Emotional Dog and Its Rational Tail: A Social Intuitionist Approach to Moral Judgment." *Psychological Review*. Vol. 108, No. 4, 814–834.

Hamblen, Jessica, and Laurie B. Stone. 2007. "What Are the Traumatic Stress Effects of Terrorism?" National Center for PTSD Fact Sheet. Available online at www.ncptsd.va.gov.

Hardin, Garrett. 1968. "The Tragedy of the Commons." *Science*. Vol. 162, No. 3852, p. 1243-1248.

Hauser, Marc D. 2007. *Moral Minds: The Nature of Right and Wrong*. New York, NY: Harper.

Hayek, Friedrich A. 1960. *The Constitution of Liberty*. Chicago, IL: University of Chicago Press.

_____. 1952. *The Sensory Order*. Chicago, IL: University of Chicago Press.

Hebb, Donald M. 1949. *The Organization of Behavior: A Neuropsychological Theory*. New York, NY: John Wiley & Sons.

Hobbs, Thomas. 1965. *Leviathan or The Matter, Forme and Power of a Commonwealth Ecclesiastical and Civil*. Michael Oaskeshott, ed. Oxford, UK: Basil Blackwell. Originally published in 1651.

Huntington, Samuel P. 1996. *The Clash of Civilizations and the Remaking of the World Order*. New York, NY: Simon and Schuster.

Hutcheson, Francis. 1725. *An Inquiry into the Origin of our Ideas of Beauty and Virtue; in Two Treatises*. London: J. Darby. Yale University Library Collection.

Iacoboni, Marco, and Mirella Dapretto. 2006. "The Mirror Neuron System and the Consequences of Its Dysfunction." *Nature Reviews Neuroscience*. Vol. 7, December, 942–951.

Kagel, John H., and Alvin E. Roth. 1995. *The Handbook of Experimental Economics*. Princeton, NJ: Princeton University Press.

Kendall-Tackett, Kathleen A. 2000. "Physiological Correlates of Childhood Abuse: Chronic Hyperarousal in PTSD, Depression, and Irritable Bowel Syndrome." *Child Abuse & Neglect*. Vol. 24, 799–810.

Kindleberger, Charles P. 1996 [1978]. *Manias, Panics, and Crashes: A History of Financial Crises*. New York, NY: John Wiley & Sons.

Koenigs, Michael, and Daniel Tranel. 2007. "Irrational Decision Making After Ventromedial Prefrontal Damage: Evidence from the Ultimatum Game." *The Journal of Neuroscience*. January 24, Vol. 27, No. 4, 951–956.

LeDoux, Joseph. 2002. *The Synaptic Self: How Our Brains Become Who We Are*. New York, NY: Penguin.

_____. 1996. *The Emotional Brain: The Mysterious Underpinnings of Emotional Life*. New York, NY: Simon and Schuster.

Lieberman, Matthew D., and Naomi I. Eisenberger. 2006. "A Pain By Any Other Name (Rejection, Exclusion, Ostracism) Still Hurts the Same: The Role of Dorsal Anterior Cingulate Cortex in Social and Physical Pain." In Cacioppo, John T., Penny S. Visser, and Cynthia L. Pickett. 2006. *Social Neuroscience: People Thinking About Thinking People*. Cambridge, MA: MIT Press.

Liu, Andrew C., David K. Welsh, Caroline H. Ko, Hien G. Tran, Eric E. Zhang, Aaron A Priest, Ethen D. Butler, Oded Singer, Kirsten Meeker, Inder M. Verma, Francis J. Doyle III, Joseph S. Takahashi, and Steve A. Kay. 2007. "Intercellular Coupling Confers Robustness Against Mutations, in the SCN Circadian Clock Network." *Cell*, Vol. 129, 605-616, May 4.

McCabe, Kevin. 2006. "The Neuroeconomics of Personal and Interpersonal Decision Making." In De Crimer, David, Marcel Zulenberg, and J. Keith Murnigham, eds. 2006. *Social Psychology and Economics*. Mahwah, NJ: Lawrence Erlbaum Associates.

_____. 2003. "Neuroeconomics." In Lynn Nadel, Editor in Chief. 2003. *Encyclopedia of Cognitive Science*. Nature Publishing Group, Macmillan Publishers. Vol. 3, 294–298.

McCabe, Kevin, Daniel Houser, Lee Ryan, Vernon Smith, and Theodore Trouard. 2001. "A Functional Imaging Study of 'Theory of Mind' in Two-Person Reciprocal Exchange." *Proceedings of the National Academy of Sciences*. 98, 11832–11835.

McNally, Richard J. 2006. "Cognitive Abnormalities in Post Traumatic Stress Disorder." *Trends in Cognitive Sciences*. Vol. 10, No. 6, June.

Maddison, Angus. 2005. "Evidence Submitted to the Select Committee for Economic Affairs, House of Lords, London, for the 'Inquiry into Aspects of the Economics of Climate Change.'" February 20.

Malik, Saima, Francis McGlone, Diane Bedrossian, and Alain Dagher. 2008. "Ghrelin Modulates Brain Activity in Areas that Control Appetitive Behavior." *Cell Metabolism,* 7, 400-409, May.

_____. 2004. "The Contours of the World Economy and the Art of Macro-Measurement 1500-2001." Ruggles Lecture, IARIW 28th General Conference, Cork, Ireland, August.

_____. 1997a. "Causal Influences on Productivity Performance 1820–1992: A Global Perspective." *Journal of Productivity Analysis.* November. 325–360.

_____. 1997b. "The Nature and Functioning of European Capitalism: A Historical and Comparative Perspective." *Banca Nazionale del Lavoro Quarterly Review.* December.

_____. 1991. *Dynamic Forces in Capitalist Development.* Oxford, UK: Oxford University Press.

_____. 1982. *Economic Epochs and Their Interpretation.* Oxford, UK: Oxford University Press.

Madison, James. In Cooke, Jacob E., ed. 1961. *The Federalist.* Middletown, CT: Wesleyan University Press. Originally published February 6, 1788.

Mandeville, Bernard. 1723. *The Fable of the Bees; Or, Private Vices, Publick Benefits.* London: E. Parker. Yale University Library Collection.

Mitchell, Jason P., Malia F. Mason, C. Neil Macrae, and Mahzerin R. Banaji. 2006. "Thinking About Others: The Neural Substrates of Social Cognition." In Cacioppo, John T., Penny S. Visser, and Cynthia L. Pickett. 2006. *Social Neuroscience: People Thinking About Thinking People*. Cambridge, MA: MIT Press.

National Institute of Mental Health. 2007. "Cell Networking Keeps Brain's Master Clock Ticking." Science Update, May 4. At www.nimh.nih.gov.

Niebur, Ernst, Steven S. Hsiao, and Kenneth O. Johnson. "Synchrony: a Neuronal Mechanism for Attentional Selection?" 2002. *Current Opinion in Neurobiology*. 23:190-194.

Nemeroff, Charles B., J. Douglas Bremner, Edna B. Foa, Helen S. Mayberg, Carol S. North, and Murray B. Stein. 2006. "Post Traumatic Stress Disorder: A State-of-the-Science Review." *Journal of Psychiatric Research*. 40: 1–21.

Nolte, John. 1999. *The Human Brain: An Introduction to Its Functional Anatomy*. Fourth Edition. St. Louis, MO: Mosby.

North, Douglass C. 2005. *Understanding the Process of Economic Change*. Princeton, NJ: Princeton University Press.

North, Douglass C., John Joseph Wallis, and Barry R. Weingast. Forthcoming. *Violence and Social Orders: A Conceptual Framework for Interpreting Recorded Human History*. Cambridge, UK: Cambridge University Press.

Ochsner, Kevin N. 2006. "Characterizing the Functional Architecture of Affect Regulation: Emerging Answers and Outstanding Questions." In Cacioppo, John T., Penny S. Visser, and Cynthia L. Pickett. 2006. *Social Neuroscience: People Thinking About Thinking People*. Cambridge, MA: MIT Press.

Ochsner, Kevin N., Silvia A. Bunge, James J. Gross, and John D. Gabrieli. 2005. "Rethinking Feelings: An fMRI Study of the Cognitive Regulation of Emotion." In Cacioppo, John T. and Gary G. Berntson, eds. 2005. *Social Neuroscience*. New York, NY: Psychology Press.

Orwell, George. 1949. *1984*. New York, NY: Milestone Editions.

Oren, Michael. 2007. *Power, Faith, and Fantasy: America in the Middle East 1776 to the Present*. New York, NY: W.W. Norton & Co.

Ostrom, Elinor. 1990. *Governing the Commons: The Evolution of Institutions for Collective Action*. Cambridge, UK: Cambridge University Press.

Ostrom, Elinor, and Harini Nagendra. 2006. "Insights on Linking Forests, Trees, and People from the Air, on the Ground, and in the Laboratory." *Proceedings of the National Academy of Sciences*. Vol. 103, No. 51, 19224–19231. December 19.

Ostrom, Elinor, Roy Gardner, and James Walker. 1994. *Rules, Games, and Common-Pool Resources*. Ann Arbor, MI: University of Michigan Press.

Ostrom, Vincent. 1972. "Polycentricity." Presented at the Annual Meeting of the American Political Science Association, Washington, D.C., September 5–9. Reprinted in: McGinnis, Michael, ed. 1999. "Polycentricity and Local Public Economies: Readings from the Workshop in Political Theory and Policy Analysis." Ann Arbor, MI: University of Michigan Press.

Ostrom, Vincent, Charles M. Tiebout, and Robert Warren. 1961. "The Organization of Government in Metropolitan Areas: A Theoretical Inquiry." *The American Political Science Review*. Vol. 55, Issue 4, 831–842. December.

Paz, Octavio. 1969. *Conjunctions and Disjunctions*. New York, NY: Grove Press.

Pinker, Stephen. 1997. *How the Mind Works*. New York, NY: W.W. Norton.

Polski, Margaret M., and Elinor Ostrom. 1999. "An Institutional Framework for Policy Analysis and Design." Workshop in Political Theory and Policy Analysis Working Paper W98-27. Indiana University, Bloomington, IN.

Posner, Michael J., and Marcus E. Raichle. 1997. *Images of the Mind*. New York, NY: Scientific American Library.

Raichle, Marcus E. 2006. "Social Neuroscience: A Perspective." In Cacioppo, John T., Penny S. Visser, and Cynthia L. Pickett. 2006. *Social Neuroscience: People Thinking About Thinking People*. Cambridge, MA: MIT Press.

Raichle, Marcus E., Ann Mary Macleod, Abraham Z. Snyder, William J. Powers, Debra A. Gasnard, and Gordon L. Shulman. 2001. "A Default Mode of Brain Function." Proceedings of the National Academy of Sciences. Inaugural Article Neurobiology: 98: 2: 676–682. January 16.

Rausch, Scot L., Lisa M. Shin, and Elizabeth A. Phelps. 2006. "Neurocircuitry Models of Post Traumatic Stress Disorder and Extinction: Human Neuroimaging Research—Past, Present and Future." *Biological Psychiatry*. 60: 376–382.

Rubenstein, Ariel. 2008. "Comments on Neuroeconomics." *Economics and Philosophy.*Version March 9.

Sanfey, Alan G., James K. Rilling, Jessica A. Aronson, Leigh E. Nystrom, and Jonathan D. Cohen. 2003. "The Neural Basis of Economic Decision Making in the Ultimatum Game." *Science*. June 13. Vol. 300.

Schacter, Daniel. 2001. *The Seven Sins of Memory*. New York, NY: Houghton Mifflin.

Schelling, Thomas C.. 2005. "An Astonishing Sixty Years: The Legacy of Hiroshima." Nobel Prize Lecture. December 8.

_____. 1980. *The Strategy of Conflict*. Cambridge, MA: Harvard University Press.

Schneier, Bruce. 2007. "The Psychology of Security." Working Paper. February 28.

Schultz, Wolfram. 2000. "Multiple Reward Signals in the Brain." *Nature Reviews Neuroscience*. Vol. 1, 189–207.

Simon, Herbert A. 1957. *Models of Man: Social and Rational*. New York, NY: John Wiley & Sons.

Simon, Herbert A., and Albert Newell. 1964. "Information Processing in Computer and Man." *American Scientist*. 52: 281–300.

Singer, Tania, Daniel Wolpert, and Chris Firth. "Introduction: The Study of Social Interactions." In Firth, Christopher D., and Daniel M. Wolpert, eds. 2003. *The Neuroscience of Social Interaction: Decoding, Imitating, and Influencing the Actions of Others*. Oxford, England: Oxford University Press.

Smith, Adam. 1976 [1776]. *An Inquiry into the Nature and Causes of the Wealth of Nations*. Chicago, IL: University of Chicago Press.

_____. 1759. *The Theory of Moral Sentiments*. Printed for A. Millar in the Strand and A. Kincaid and J. Bell in Edinburgh, Scotland. Reprinted in Smith, Adam. 1982. *The Theory of Moral Sentiments*. Indianapolis, Indiana: The Liberty Fund.

Smith, Vernon. L. 2003. "Constructivist and Ecological Rationality in Economics." *The American Economic Review*. Vol. 93, No. 3, 465–508.

_____. 1997. "The Two Faces of Adam Smith." Southern Economic Association Distinguished Guest Lecture, Atlanta, Georgia. November 21.

_____. 1994. "Economics in the Laboratory." *Journal of Economic Perspectives*. Vol. 8, No. 1, Winter, 113–131.

_____. 1989. "Theory, Experiment and Economics." *Journal of Economic Perspectives*. Vol. 3, No. 1, Winter, 151–169.

_____. 1982. "Microeconomic Systems as an Experimental Science." *The American Economic Review*. 72: 5: 923–955.

Stocco, Andrea and Danilo Fum. 2007. "Implicit Emotional Biases in Decision Making: The Case of the Iowa Gambling Task." *Brain and Cognition*, 66, 253-259.

Tsien, Joe Z. 2007a. "The Memory Code (extended version)." *Scientific American*. June 17.

_____. 2007b. "The Memory Code." *Scientific American*. July.

Vasterling, Jennifer J. 2007. "PTSD and Neurocognition." *PTSD Research Quarterly*. Vol. 18, No. 1, Winter.

Wood, Jacqueline N., and Jordan Grafman. 2003. "Human Prefrontal Cortex: Processing and Representational Perspectives." *Nature Review Neuroscience*. Vol. 4, February, 139–147.

Endnotes

Introduction

1. Schelling (2005).

Chapter 1

1. Maddison (2004).

2. The Economist (2006).

3. Maddison (2005).

4. The "no strings" policy works as follows. In return for recognizing that Taiwan is part of China, China will provide economic assistance to a country with no conditions on the terms of investment or trade. This is contrary to the policies of international financial institutions and developed country assistance programs, which all impose conditions that require the recipient country to observe standards set by developed countries.

5. North, Wallis, and Weingast (forthcoming).

6. Maddison (1982).

7. Perhaps best known for *The Leviathan*, his treatise on the rationale for government, Hobbes argued that in the "state of nature," our primary goal is survival. Faced with scarcity that leads to constant conflict and abject misery, we recognize that it is in

our material self-interest to enter into a social contract with an absolute authority (a "Leviathan") that can secure peace and provide a common defense.

8. Building on the work of Bacon and Descartes, prominent contributions to this bubbling caldron of new thinking include Bentham, Hobbes, Hume, Locke, Montesquieu, Rousseau, and Voltaire.

9. The eighteenth-century version of this debate in England was launched by the moralist Bernard Mandeville. Taking issue with the reformers of the day who railed against the vice and social ill that accompanied growth and urged strict self-governance and virtuous asceticism, Mandeville argued instead for individual liberty and strong, mitigating government. In a rejoinder, Francis Hutchison (Adam Smith's teacher and mentor) argued that strong government is not needed to achieve virtuous ends because human nature is inherently benevolent and rational.

10. Often overlooked, Smith's treatise on human nature, *The Theory of Moral Sentiments*, is, in my view, essential to developing a complete understanding of his ideas on political economy, which are explained in *The Wealth of Nations*.

11. Maddison (1997b).

12. Oren (2007).

13. Madison, 51 in Cooke, Ed. (1961).

14. The "tragedy of the commons," popularized by Garrett Hardin in his 1968 *Science* essay by the same name, refers to the conflict of individual and common interests over non-renewable resources. Hardin argued that allowing the "invisible hand" of self-governed exchange to freely operate will doom a resource to extinction because people cannot restrain themselves from over-exploitation. The inevitability of this result has been roundly

disputed by Elinor Ostrom (1990) and Ostrom, Gardnes, and Walker (1994), who provide evidence that people are often (but not always) able to reconcile individual and common interests and effectively regulate themselves to sustain a wide range of common pool resources.

15. For an overview of contemporary research in this field, see Glimcher, et al. (2008).

16. North (2005).

Chapter 2

1. There is considerable evidence that humans are able to develop new neural connections throughout life. For an overview of brain plasticity, see Gazzaniga, et al. (2002, Chapter 15). For a range of contemporary research perspectives, see Gazzaniga, ed. (2004, Part II). For a more readily accessible account, see Doidge (2007).

2. For an overview, see Wolford, Miller, and Gazzaniga (2004) in Gazzaniga, ed. (2004, Part X, 85). Also see Gazzaniga (2005 and 1998).

3. For a review of the literature, see Kendall-Taggett (2000).

4. For recent reviews of the literature on PTSD, see Hamblen and Stone (2007), Vasterling (2007), Nemeroff, et al. (2006), McNally (2006), and Rausch, et al. (2006).

Chapter 3

1. Gazzaniga, et al. (2002) attribute the concept of "theory of mind" to David Premack. See the interview with David Premack (p. 676–677).

2. Crick (1994).

3. Liu, et al. (2007) and National Institute of Mental Health (2007). Similarly, Malik, et al. (2008) find evidence that the neural signaling associated with our appetite for food arises from interacting cues in our environment, our gut, and our brain.

4. Wood and Grafman (2003) describe how the prefrontal cortex is organized, its role in thinking and choice, and review theories of how it functions.

Chapter 4

1. Damasio (1999, 2003).

2. Raichle, et al. (2001).

3. See, for example, McCabe, et al. (2001), Sanfey, et al. (2003), and Stocco and Fum (2007).

4. See, for example, Koenig and Tranel (2007). For a review of the literature on the ventromedial prefrontal cortex and the role of social and emotional regulation in decision making, see Wood and Grafman (2003).

Chapter 5

1. As cited in Curtis and Greenslet, eds. (1962).

2. Doidge (2007) attributes this expression to Carla Shatz.

3. Tsien (2007).

4. See Damasio (1999, 1994).

5. Barsalou, et al. (2003).

6. See, for example, Barsalou, et al. (2003) and Cacioppo and Berntson, eds. (2005).

7. Edelman (2006).

8. Schneier (2007).

9. Cacioppo and Berntson, eds. (2005).

Chapter 6

1. Lieberman and Eisenberger (2006).

2. Gusnard (2006).

3. Barsalou, et al. (2003).

4. For a review of the literature, see Iacoboni, et al. (2006).

5. Gallese (2007).

6. Those who are familiar with the framework for institutional analysis and development developed in the Workshop in Political Theory and Policy Analysis at Indiana University will find a familiar core in this concept. Also see Polski and E. Ostrom (1999) and E. Ostrom, et al. (1994).

Chapter 7

1. Rubenstein (2008).

2. Huntington (1996).

3. E. Ostrom (2007). Dr. Ostrom founded the Center for the Study of Institutions, Population, and Environmental Change at Indiana University, and she is a Co-Director of the Center for the Study of Institutional Diversity in the School of Human Evolution and Social Change at Arizona State University.

4. For a detailed description of current military thinking about irregular warfare, see Irregular Warfare Joint Operating Concept, Department of Defense, Version 1.0, September 11, 2007. Available at www.fas.org/irp/doddir/dod/iw-joc.pdf. For early and influential work on the topic, see Galua (1963) and Liddel Hart (1967) and (1960).

5. Donahue and Fenzel (2008).

6. The evidence for asset bubbles is overwhelming, and if you think about it, they may be what makes investment lucrative and interesting: If the efficient market hypothesis was achievable, there would be few reasons to invest in anything but a sure thing, much less capital available for investment, and slower economic growth. Current research focuses on finding trading rules that can dampen bubbles and lesson the effects of contagion. For early and influential work in this area, see Kindleberger (1996 [1978]) and the theoretical work of Diamond and Dybvig (1983). For compendiums of the experimental evidence on asset trading, see Davis and Holt (1993) and Kagel and Roth (1995).

7. For the full report, see Interim Report of the Committee on Capital Markets Regulation, November 30, 2006. Available at www.capmktsreg.org.

8. V. Ostrom (1972) and V. Ostrom, et al. (1961). For applications to dealing with terrorism, see Frey (2004).

INDEX